ESSENTIAL
CORVETTE
STING RAY

ESSENTIAL
CORVETTE
STING RAY

THE CARS AND THEIR STORY
1963-67

TOM FALCONER

SPECIAL PHOTOGRAPHY BY BERLE CHERNEY

Published 1995 by Bay View Books Ltd
The Red House, 25-26 Bridgeland Street,
Bideford, Devon EX39 2PZ, UK

Reprinted 1996
Reprinted 1998

Edited by Mark Hughes
Typesetting and design by Chris Fayers & Sarah Ward

ISBN 1 870979 62 1
Printed in Hong Kong

Corvette, Sting Ray, Vette and GM are registered trade marks of General Motors Corporation.

CONTENTS

CORVETTE'S FIRST TEN YEARS

How could it possibly happen that General Motors Corporation, for the past 85 years the world's largest manufacturer of motor vehicles, could build for more than 40 of those years a limited-production sports car made of fiberglass? And how could it be that GM, for almost all of this time the world's largest manufacturing corporation of any description, and one that has always been ruthlessly efficient in its successful pursuit of a profit every quarter for its shareholders, could make and sell a car that has lost money for most of its life? Is it really likely that a handful of car fanatics working in senior positions in a corporation that is notorious for employing non-automotive people could have had the influence required to make this enduring

The 1953 Corvette was Chevrolet's first attempt at building a two-seater sports car, pioneering the fiberglass construction that became an enduring Corvette feature, lasting to the present day.

two-seater the most successful sports car of all time?

The Corvette has an interesting and unlikely story, the whole truth of which will never be known. What is certain, however, is that Chevrolet in 1953 was the dullest of the American car makers. It specialized in selling trouble-free cars to the kind of people who did not even like them, those who would always say that a car's purpose was just to get from A to B, with no thrill or driver satisfaction – people who never chose the old

All 1954 Corvettes used the asthmatic six-cylinder motor and two-speed automatic transmission: performance did not match appearance (above). A 1961 Corvette (right), powered by the last of the 283 engines: Corvette was both the first and last production car to feature a full wrap-around windshield.

twisting road simply because it was more fun.

Boring they may have been, but Chevrolets still had to be sold and promoted. Starting in 1949, GM had instigated a series of travelling exhibitions to show to the public not only the latest production models from the five Car Divisions, but also the futuristic dream cars that were being turned out by the Styling Section. This was a time of extraordinary economic growth, optimism about the future, full employment and faith in the promise of technology to improve everyone's future wealth and lifestyle. Initially called 'Transportation Unlimited' in 1949 and '50, the show was relaunched in 1953 as the 'General Motors Motorama' after a two-year break during the Korean War. Visiting six major cities and

carried on a large fleet of specially-built trucks, the cars were presented on elaborate stages with singers and dancers. By the end of the last Motorama show in 1961, more than 10 million people had visited them, and many had been interviewed by market researchers to glean opinion on the cars shown.

The first Corvette was built as a fully working Dream Car for the 1953 Motorama, and the man who conceived it was the head of styling, Harley Earl. The son of a Los Angeles coachbuilder who had pushed his father's business into building elaborate customized cars for the new Hollywood movie stars, Earl had come to Detroit to design the first 1927 La Salle – the affordable Cadillac. GM President Alfred Sloan hired Earl to head a new 'Art

The Motorama Corvette, the first of the line (above). Although it might look staid to modern eyes, this was a dazzling styling statement in 1953.

Corvette went on to become the world's best-selling sports car ever. Body drop at Chevrolet's St Louis plant (right), the moment when a 1958 Corvette becomes a car.

and Colour' section, which in due course became the Styling Staff – colour was spelt with the English 'u' to make the department sound more stylish! It was Harley Earl who gave the 1949 Cadillac its fins, which went on to grow annually for 12 years, and who interpreted into metal the perceived stratification of the five Car Divisions, from lofty and opulent Cadillac to lowly but good-value Chevrolet.

Earl picked Bob McLean to design a car for the 1953 Motorama. The brief was to use as many production components as possible and to seat two people in the style of the British Jaguar XK120, a car that was already selling well in the US after its 1949 introduction. Design work started in April 1951, with the intention that the car should be as cheap as a Chevrolet sedan. Under the

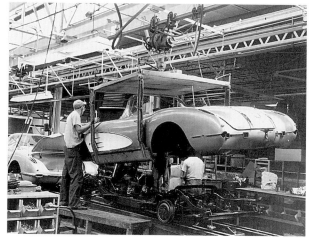

hood it was decided to use the Chevrolet straight-six engine, tuned with triple carburetors to give 150bhp.

The only other performance engine that GM had available was the short-stroke, high-compression Cadillac 331cu in V8 introduced in 1949. This advanced production motor had powered a two-door Coupe de Ville to 10th position at the Le Mans 24 Hours race in

Sketch by Larry Shinoda for the Mako Shark (above). GM attracted, and kept, the very best stylists and used their talents to the full. Shinoda was involved in the styling of the Sting Ray racer and went on to be largely responsible for the '63 Corvette Sting Ray, and the later '68 Corvette. Bill Mitchell (left), always immaculately attired, discusses '63 Corvette styling ideas with Irv Rybicki and Bill Tochman. More than anyone else, Mitchell was determined that the Corvette should be a great looking car.

1950, entered by Briggs Cunningham and driven by Miles and Sam Collier. Legend has it that they kept themselves awake during the night by listening on the car radio to jazz transmitted by the American Forces Network! Although these Cadillac V8s were also fitted into the engineless sports cars shipped over by the English Allard company, it was perceived knowledge in those days that sports cars had to be fitted with an engine having four or six cylinders.

It is fair to speculate that had this engine been chosen, then the Corvette would have been a Cadillac Corvette and the histories of both Cadillac and Chevrolet since 1953 would have been quite different. It is also fair to say that the 1953 and '54 Corvettes would have been much better cars.

McLean's design was radical by the standards of the time. He gave the Corvette nifty wire screens over recessed headlamps when all other production cars had a pop-eyed look, and he incorporated Harley Earl's wrap-

With the Corvette SS racer (left) are Ed Cole on the left, key man behind both the Corvette and the Chevrolet small-block V8, and engineer Zora Arkus-Duntov, who turned a dream car into a sports car. Bill Mitchell's Sting Ray racer of 1959 (below left), source of the 1963-67 Corvette shape, during its red period. The car was based on the chassis of the 1957 Corvette SS 'Mule', which was bought from GM for $500.

around windshield, an industry first that was previewed on the 1951 Le Sabre Dream car. The body was a simple and organic shape, emphasized by the projecting tail lights. Time was short and a completely new chassis frame had to be designed. Probably because it would have taken too long to perfect clutch and shifter linkages, the Corvette was fitted with an automatic transmission, a decision that was seriously to compromise its sporty image.

The Motorama Corvette prototype was built with a fiberglass body: in keeping with the image that GM was trying to project in this futuristic show, there were plenty of column inches of publicity to be derived from showing a plastic car that could not rust. The public reception of the car was overwhelmingly positive – there was obviously a market for the Corvette.

While the car had been designed for the body alternatively to be in steel, there were advantages to taking the plastic route. The fiberglass body would need much cheaper tooling than the alternative steel one, in fact less than one tenth of the cost, and the molds could be ready in six months rather than a year. Taking

advantage of the waves of good publicity generated by the Motorama Corvette, the decision was taken to start limited production with the plastic body.

A pilot plant was set up at Flint, Michigan, and orders were placed with suppliers to build 300 cars. Unfortunately, this sporty new Chevrolet turned out to be very expensive to build and was finally stickered at $3734, more than twice the cost of a Chevrolet sedan and about the same as a new Cadillac. But Chevrolet still had the scarcity factor on its side, and exploited this by selling the cars to VIPs and celebrities on an invitation-only basis. Although the cars looked terrific, and were easy to drive with their automatic transmissions, they were no substitute for an Eldorado. The six-cylinder motor was gutless, the triple carburetors went out of tune too easily, and worst of all there were no side windows, just side curtains that were stored in the trunk and had to be retrieved and fitted if it rained. The VIP buyers also tended to dislike the lack of outside door handles.

The hand-build line at Flint had served its purpose and was closed down. Full production in a newly-equipped part of the Chevrolet plant at St Louis began in

December 1953, building '54 models. These differed
externally from the previous year's model only in having
a beige rather than black soft-top. But it was soon
obvious that sales were poor and production for the year
was cut back to just 3640, instead of the planned 10,000.
Even so, cars piled up in the shipping area and by January
1955 a third of '54 production still remained unsold. Not
surprising, for these are truly awful cars – with apologies
to present owners, who mostly trailer them if they move
them at all. They have terrific on-the-road presence, but
they are slow and dull, with terminal understeer.

At this point it is extraordinary that the experiment
was not quietly forgotten. The Corvette was saved first
by the launch of a competitor's product. Ford introduced
its 1955 Thunderbird two-seater convertible with a V8
and a choice of auto or manual transmission. If the
Dearborn manufacturer was going to open up a new
market for personal cars, then GM had to persevere with
its own contender rather than hand this potential growth

**The Sting Ray racer
photographed by the
author while in storage
at the General Motors
Tech Center in 1985 – in
motion even while
parked. This interior, in
later show car guise, was** **fitted following the car's
retirement from racing at
the end of 1960. The first
Mako Shark show car
(below), based on a solid-
axle Corvette, was a
teaser to presage the new
production Sting Ray.**

sector to its arch rival. The new T-Bird was a very good car, sweet handling, powerful and beautifully thought out. It even had glass side windows with power lifts and a detachable hard-top.

In addition the Corvette was transformed by replacing the old 'stovebolt' six with the new 'small-block' 265cu in, 195bhp Chevrolet V8, an outstanding engine designed by a team led by chief engineer Ed Cole. Having joined Chevrolet in 1952, Cole was one of the prime movers behind the Corvette. Previously he had been at Cadillac, again as chief engineer, where he had been the man behind the new 331cu in V8. Given the chance to have a second go at an all-new V8, he went all out for simplicity and lightness.

Cole's team delivered the motor which would power Corvettes – and other Chevrolets – for the next 40-plus years. It would not only become the most popular car engine ever built, but also the most successful performance engine. Since a 'mule' was needed for engineering development and for testing the V8, the old Motorama dream car was pulled out of retirement, the six removed and the new motor installed. It was then given 25,000 miles of endurance testing at the Milford Proving Ground, the 6-volt electrics were heaved out in favor of 12-volt, and the car was approved for 1955 production. The stylists designed a large letter 'V', which fitted over the small 'v' in the maker's name on the front fender, to signify to the world that the car at last had the power it needed to kick its tail out. The Corvette now had a power to weight ratio worthy of a sports car. The Motorama show car, experimental car EX122, was eventually sold off as just another used Corvette, and still exists today.

The V8 was some 40lb lighter than the six but had a 40bhp advantage. Better still, 10 per cent of the 700 '55 cars that were built also received a clutch and a three-speed manual transmission, redeeming the car in the eyes of traditional sports car fans. A few were raced as well – the revised Corvette clearly had promise.

Two larger-than-life characters now arrived on the scene and would help set the Corvette back on course. The first was the engineer Zora Arkus-Duntov. Born in Belgium in 1909, he had Russian parents and was raised in Russia, studying engineering at Leningrad University. After graduation he went to work on a number of automotive projects in Germany and Belgium before arriving in New York in 1940. There he opened a machine shop with his brother Yuri, and after spending the war years on military projects he designed and built the famous Ardun overhead valve aluminum cylinder

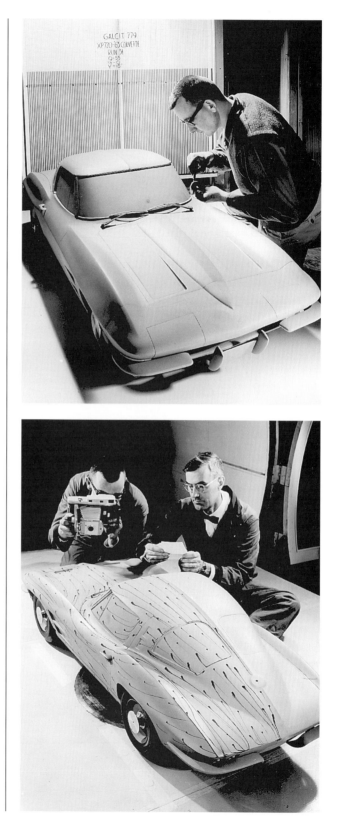

Refining the design. Kent Kelly fixes a mirror to a superbly detailed model of the split-window coupe prior to aerodynamic testing (facing page, top), and photographs it with an early Polaroid camera after a wind tunnel session, with Dr Kyropoulos checking one of the instant prints (facing page, bottom). Pre-production prototype with the original racer on the hallowed hexagonal tiles of the outside styling viewing area (right).

head conversion for the flathead Ford V8. These were used by the English Allard sports car company, for whom he then went to work and race drive until 1952. Returning to America, and by now vastly experienced in many aspects of automotive engineering, he started work at Chevrolet in 1953 and soon found his way on to the Corvette program.

Having such a skilled engineer who doubled as a successful racing driver was the magic combination that the Corvette needed. By 1956 he had perfected the famous Duntov long-duration cam for the small block, organized a record-breaking run with three cars on Daytona Beach (personally managing a two-way average speed of 150.583mph), and assisted in the design of the 1957 Corvette fuel injection. Rightly credited as the father of the Corvette, he is an amusing raconteur with an energetic enthusiasm for fast cars and an almost incomprehensible accent. On a personal note, I value my lunch with him back in 1982 as one of the great moments of my own time with Corvettes.

The second great character who would play a key role in the Sting Ray's development was Bill Mitchell. A true car fanatic, he had joined Harley Earl's styling team in 1936, having started out as an illustrator at the Barron Collier advertising agency in New York. He was first

introduced to motor racing by Barron Collier's three sons, who had their own small race track at the Collier country estate; the younger two sons were Sam and Miles, who would race their Cadillac at Le Mans in 1950. Through them Mitchell was indirectly introduced to Earl, who on his retirement years later, in December 1958, personally picked him as his successor as vice-president in charge of design. Ultimately responsible for the design and styling of more than ten million cars, Mitchell devoted his energy to the Corvette over his entire career until his retirement in 1976.

I was fortunate to corner him for an interview in London in 1984. Although obviously enjoying his retirement, he was still deeply interested in motor vehicles and full of the pithy, down-home philosophy for which he was renowned while doing his rounds of the studios, or fighting for a favorite project in the boardroom. In his own words, he had gasoline in his blood, an absolute passion for fast and great-looking cars. A big and tall man, his pursuit of style had brought him to London to see his tailor. While at GM he loved to be photographed in his latest automotive creations, often in a suit to match the color of the car. He did this as much to annoy his staid fellow board members as to please himself. It was easy to see how his zest for life had

GM has always produced fabulous photographs to promote its cars (facing page). The clear detail around the gas filler and the top of the door reveal this to be a prototype of the split-window coupe. Outside the Styling building at

Tech Center (above), Bill Mitchell and friends with his Sting Ray racer that started it all. This photo was probably taken in 1962: both '63 cars at left have early two-eared wheel spinners and the red convertible has special front fender vents.

enthused his staff, and how this made the Corvette into the car he wanted.

Mitchell restyled the Corvette to make it one of the great designs of the 1950s, giving it the scooped-out cove, usually in a contrasting color, between the front wheel and the middle of the door. But by 1958 the car that anticipated the shape of the '63 Sting Ray was already starting to take shape in the styling fabrication shop. Mitchell had managed to buy from Chevrolet the chassis of the 'Mule', the test car from the cancelled SS racing program, of which more later, and it was to be the basis of his own racing car. Larry Shinoda worked with his boss on the project, which took its cues from another abandoned venture, Bob McLean's Corvette Q.

As a GM vice-president, Mitchell could propel a

project such as this, and his new car – which he called the Sting Ray – raced first at Marlboro, Maryland, in April 1959 with Dick Thompson driving. In 1960 they went on to win their class in the SCCA National Championship. With no sponsorship and only unofficial and unauthorized assistance from GM, this was some achievement, paid for from Mitchell's own pocket.

Mitchell then decided he could no longer afford to race, and in 1961 the car was sold back to GM and rebuilt as a show car. As a racer it had suffered from aerodynamic lift, which we now know to have been because of its airplane wing shape in cross-section. But lift in cars was not well understood then and this trait was to remain a problem for the production Corvette Sting Ray for any driver exceeding 120mph.

GM knows how to make the transfer from one model to another without alienating its customers. In all the major body change-overs, the base and any optional engines have always been carried over from old to new. Additionally, to smooth the transition to the Sting Ray, whose body shape was finalised by 1960, the '61 and '62 models were given a new tail shape resembling the style chosen for the '63 car, with the same tail lamp treatment. However, the '62 remains the last model with an externally accessed trunk.

THE NEW STING RAY

Launched in September 1962, the new 1963 Sting Ray was an immediate hit with almost everyone who saw it. There were crowds in the showrooms, full order books and long delivery times quoted by the dealers. The press raved about the car, fuelling enthusiasm and demand. Schoolboys persuaded their dads to buy them, club racers bought them for the circuits, and people who just loved beautiful cars bought them because they looked so good.

The Corvette had successfully made the transition from an early 1950s sports car into a mid-1960s supersports car, and with the fully enclosed split-window

One of the 26 September 1962 press release pictures from the era when air travel was still glamorous. This car is a prototype, with hand-built windshield moldings and wheel spinners facing in the wrong direction.

coupe Chevrolet could now compete with the world's best GT cars. Today the single best feature of the Corvette is its non-rusting fiberglass body, the essence of the car that preserves it for us to enjoy 30-plus years later. But to the new car buyer the body material was, and is, of little consequence – even today many buyers of new

Two pre-production pilot-line '63s on the banking at GM's Milford Proving Ground in Michigan (left). These cars are fitted with prototype P-48 knock-off aluminum wheels, with the early two-eared spinners – production cars in '63 always had three-eared spinners. The '63 Corvette as seen in that year's Chevrolet full-range brochure (below), almost the last in which color renderings were used in preference to photographs.

NEW CORVETTE
TWO NEW CLASSIC LOOKS FOR AMERICA'S SPORTS CAR—New aerodynamic styling distinguishes two totally new models—the swept-back Sport Coupe and sleek new Convertible. Rich bucket seat interior is complemented by a cockpit-cluster console, deep-twist carpeting and many other standard luxury features. Standard power team: 250-hp Corvette V8 with 3-Speed Synchro-Mesh. Other optional* engines (up to the 360-hp Ramjet Fuel Injection V8) are available, plus 4-Speed Synchro-Mesh* and Powerglide* transmissions. For full information, see the New Corvette Catalog.

Corvette Sting Ray Sport Coupe in Daytona Blue.

Corvettes have no idea that they are driving a plastic car. The only real benefit bestowed on the first owner by the plastic body was the better residual value at trade-in time, but the advantages for later owners such as you or me are almost immeasurable. You can, however, measure the width of your self-satisfied smile when you see friends trying to cut the rust out of their steel-bodied cars…

The buyer of a new car sells within two to five years and is less technically aware than subsequent owners. This buyer is very influenced by appearance and image, and it was this that GM targeted when it made its new Corvette so beautiful. Like Ferrari, GM knows that performance cars will not sell unless they look as good as they go.

Engine choices......................................

As has happened at both of the subsequent new body shape launches, in 1968 and 1984, the engine range was carried over from the previous year with no changes. The base engine, with 250bhp, remained the 327cu in, which had eight 10.25:1 pistons in 4in bores with a forged crankshaft sweeping a 3.25in stroke, and breathed through a four-barrel Carter WCFB carburetor. This nicely over-square 5.4-liter engine was the smoothest of the bunch: generally speaking all optional Corvette motors from 1956 to 1980 are more prone to vibration and mechanical noise than their standard counterparts, which deliver their best torque lower down the rev range

and are more suited to being driven in normal traffic.

Three optional engines were available for 1963. An extra $53.80 bought the most popular 1963 motor, the L75, which achieved 300bhp thanks to a larger Carter AFB carburetor, a different iron intake manifold, larger valved 'fuelie' heads, and 2⅛in outlet exhaust manifolds and exhaust system. When the two-speed automatic Powerglide transmission was specified, the 2in exhaust of the base motor was retained, but the rating remained at 300bhp. Dressed up with a partially open-element air cleaner and finned aluminum valve covers, the 340bhp L76 engine had solid lifters, the famous Duntov camshaft,

an aluminum intake manifold and a higher 11.25:1 compression ratio. While the two lower powered motors delivered their maximum at 5000rpm, the L76, like its fuel-injected version, the 360bhp L84, peaked at 6000rpm. At $107.60 the L76 option cost exactly twice as much as the 300bhp version.

Pay exactly four times that again and $430.40 bought you the same motor topped by the legendary Rochester fuel injection. First introduced in 1957 and offered in full-size Chevrolet and Pontiac sedans that year, fuel injection was dropped by Pontiac after only two years and by Chevrolet for its sedans after three years. However, the system went from strength to strength in the Corvette and was to last for nine years of production until the era of the big blocks. Unlike modern fuel injection, Rochester used no electronics but relied on a metering system that sent vacuum readings from the air intake venturi and plenum to regulate the fuel metering unit. Located on the right-hand side of the engine, the injection pump was driven by a cable from the distributor

Pre-production 1963 interior (top): full-sweep minor gauges and trip odometer in the clock were changed for production. A 1963 pilot-line coupe at the 1962 Paris Show (above).

Europeans were impressed, but punitive import duties prevented any significant sales. Even today a Corvette attracts at least 30 per cent duties in any European country.

and supplied by a conventional camshaft-driven fuel pump, as on all Chevrolet V8s.

The Corvette's comparatively light weight was ideally suited to the instant throttle response and flat torque curve of the Rochester system. Fuel injection also won favor for its economy, and for racers it meant the end of fuel starvation caused by fuel surge in the float chamber when cornering hard with carburetors. Driving a fuel-injected Corvette was a revelation to anyone brought up on the carburetor cars. Rarely exceeding 10 per cent of production, the fuel-injected cars have always been scarce. Many were stripped of their injector units and replaced with carburetors by later owners unable or unwilling to master the technology.

By any standards the performance was electrifying. A contemporary road test in the June 1957 issue of *Sports Cars Illustrated* likened the instant throttle response to a 'system of levers between the throttle pedal and your back. Press the throttle a little bit and your back is pressed NOW to the same extent. Slam the throttle down and your back is slammed NOW, even in high gear'. Later, in 1963, road testers reckoned that the fuel-injected Corvette with its 0-60mph time of only 5.6sec was bettered in acceleration only by the fabulous Mercedes-Benz 300SL, which was also fuel-injected.

For 1964 these engine options continued except that larger valves (2.02in intake, 1.60in exhaust) improved the breathing of the two top-line engines, raising their output to 365bhp and 357bhp respectively. The 365bhp used a Holley 4150 carburetor instead of the previous Carter.

With their solid lifters, the free-revving 340bhp L76 and L84 fuelie could easily exceed their 6500rpm limit, lacking the 'pump-up' effect which limits hydraulic lifter engines. As a precaution, and presumably to limit warranty claims, early 1963 cars fitted with these motors came with a tachometer which sounded a buzzer at 6500rpm. These were discontinued either because they were unnecessary or, more likely, because the buzzer could not be heard above the engine noise at full power!

Since its 1957 introduction the injection system had been developed and improved, and even used cold air induction, as an option in 1957 but standard by 1963. Today no carburetor cars are sold in America: all manufacturers have adopted fuel injection, now electronically controlled, because its superior efficiency is the key to reducing emissions.

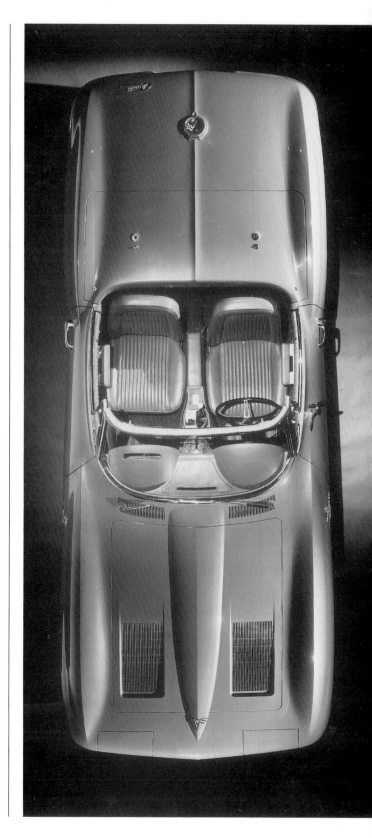

Prototype bird's eye view emphasizes subtly pinched sides – production cars had separate heater intake grilles and a different design for the fittings on the rear deck lid.

Prototype split-window coupe and roadster at a GM internal presentation, with inspirational Sting Ray racer in background (above). Both cars have vents ahead of the rear wheels – these moved to the front fenders and became functional in 1965. The author's '63 coupe (right), fitted with disc brakes, wider wheels and a five-speed Doug Nash transmission, used for years in the US in autocross, now competing in European classic rallies.

Structure & styling ....

Beneath the fiberglass body was a separate chassis fixed to it by just eight large bolts. The body was built around a fabricated steel 'birdcage' which provided the structural integrity necessary to support the door hinges and locks, and link them through the cowl and door sills to the windshield frame. On the convertible models this structure terminated at the back door pillars but on the coupe it extended across the doors and the back of the roof, making the coupe version 90 per cent stiffer. An XKE owner could remark that 90 per cent stiffer than

nothing is still nothing, but Jaguars rust and Corvettes do not. And the Jaguar restorer will never experience the thrill of removing his body from his chassis – the ultimate moment of early Corvette ownership.

No-one could pretend that the Sting Ray roadster is a stiff car. Viewed from the side with the doors open, it

A 1963 fuel-injected motor (right) – 360bhp from just 327 cubic inches.

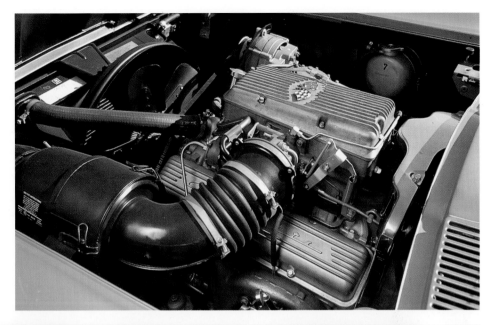

So who needs 375bhp once the tire smoke has cleared? For real driving pleasure nothing beats the torquey, low-horsepower motors such as this 1964 250bhp (below).

obviously has no cross-sectional depth compared with the deep-silled XKE, but the ease of climbing in and out is more important for most owners. Jacking the car at the recommended position just ahead of the back wheel can be an alarming experience as the door gap opens. The coupe is much stronger, even to the extent that the 'number two' body mounts on the frame rails adjacent to the transmission crossmember were omitted, leaving just three body mounts each side.

Bill Mitchell's Sting Ray racer, a vital stage in the production car's genesis, had a fabulous shape with its continuous emphasised crease around the body. But it

A 1963 300bhp motor (left) with power brakes and automatic transmission – note kickdown linkage. The stainless steel cover over the ignition system helped to prevent radio interference, a problem on a fiberglass car. Headlamps rotated by twin reversible electric motors (below) were a post-war first for an American car, enabling the striking Sting Ray racer profile to be adapted for road use.

was not easy to transform it into a road car suitable for night driving because there was nowhere for headlights of legal height to be incorporated. The solution was for the '63 to become the first post-war car with hidden headlights. Operated by individual reversible motors from a switch on the instrument panel, the headlight units incorporated thumb wheels for manual operation if required. Made of fiberglass on '63s but cast alloy thereafter, they are prone to accident damage because the divided bumpers give little protection. It used to be said of the previous Corvette that if you drove one into the wall of your home you would be claiming on your home insurance and calling a builder. Do the same in your '63 and it was sure to mean a trip to the body shop…

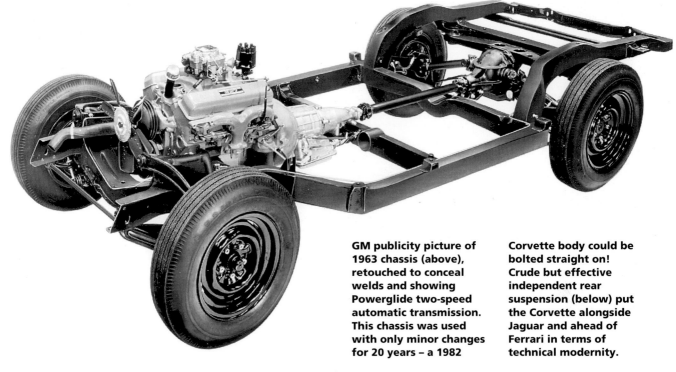

GM publicity picture of 1963 chassis (above), retouched to conceal welds and showing Powerglide two-speed automatic transmission. This chassis was used with only minor changes for 20 years – a 1982

Corvette body could be bolted straight on! Crude but effective independent rear suspension (below) put the Corvette alongside Jaguar and ahead of Ferrari in terms of technical modernity.

On the coupe the doors had extended tops which closed into a cutaway roof panel. This gave a nice airplane feel to the doors, but also brought another problem. At over 90mph the tops of the doors are pulled out by aerodynamic suction and daylight appears through the gap. If it is raining you get wet – but if you drive that fast in the rain you deserve to get wet.

The convertible continued a great Corvette tradition in having a folding roof that is fully covered by a lid when it is stowed. The installation is so neat that owners parked with the top down are constantly asked what they do when it rains – in fact the top can be raised in less than half a minute. Better still it can be lowered without getting out of the car, and with care even while driving slowly in traffic. It is a constant source of wonder to Corvette owners that it has taken other sports car marques until the 1990s to solve the problem of what to do with the top when it is down.

The roadster was available with a hard-top as a $236.75 option or in lieu of the soft-top at no extra cost. Made of fiberglass with a plexiglass back window, it has a quite different profile from the soft-top, lending the car a softer and more feminine shape. Although it still clips to the windshield header, it uses different mounting holes in the rear deck lid and additional side mountings, and is definitely a two-person job to fit. Removal of the soft-

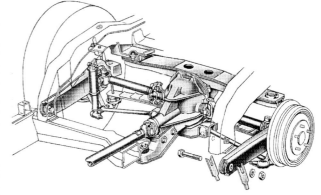

top is recommended to retain some luggage space.

The 1963 coupe body is always known as the 'split-window' because of its superb divided back window treatment. I cannot look at a 1963 coupe without settling my eyes on that gorgeous rear, and this is still the identifier for the most collectable Corvette of them all. It seems incredible now, but this feature was so reviled by most magazine writers that it was removed from the 1964 model. Contemporary articles even described how to update your '63 to the full back window. Most of the criticism cited the interior mirror blind spot which could hide a following police motorcycle – a lame excuse considering that all cars also had a door-mounted mirror.

Options ....

The door glass could be plain or tinted with the option of A31 power windows for an extra $59.20 – switches were in the centre console. The 'ventipanes' were still operated manually, even with electric windows.

Air conditioning was available for the first time on a Corvette, but only on the 250bhp and 300bhp engines. Introduced during April 1963, it was only fitted to 278 cars in the first year's production – less than two per cent. By 1967 16 per cent of cars were so fitted and this rising trend continued until 1980, when air conditioning became standard. Using a GM Frigidaire compressor, the system was nicely integrated into the design of the car, with extra ducting beneath the dash and two control knobs and an outlet grille above the clock. Because the compressor and evaporator assembly needed to be at the right-hand side of the engine, the alternator and battery were moved to the left, the battery requiring a special

Fuel-injected split-window '63 is indistinguishable from a carburetor car from the rear, but it has this front fender emblem (above):

2610 injected motors were installed in 1963. Fall colors characterize this terrific study by Berle Cherney of a '63 coupe (facing page).

Front view of the coupe (left): today's owners find it just as difficult to level the front bumpers as the factory did. A '63 coupe (below) on test with *Road & Track* magazine, who loved the new Corvette.

access panel to remove it from behind the brake booster and cylinder, while the windshield washer bottle was replaced by a flexible bag. The Corvette has always lent itself to being air conditioned, its full-size system cooling very quickly because it serves a small passenger compartment. In 1964 a three-speed blower was fitted in the left rear of the closed coupe to defog the rear window. Twin vents were incorporated in both external back window pillars.

Power steering was also a new option in 1963. Costing $75.35, it used a separate control valve and ram and was the same system that had been used on full-size Chevrolet passenger cars since 1955. At the time there was a move towards integral power steering boxes with featherlight effort which lacked the feel of the separate system. Fortunately, the Corvette engineers made the irrational choice and went for the old-fashioned system, and no-one ever complained about lack of feedback. With three separate components linked by four hoses, it is a tough system to keep leak-free but parts are cheap and available, particularly since it was used on all models through 1982. Driver expectations have changed over 30 years and now even Formula 1 cars have power steering, and there is no doubt that any Sting Ray will benefit from having power steering fitted, unless originality is of paramount concern.

Interior

The 1963 steering wheel was color-matched to the interior of the car, a fake wood rim was a late production option that became standard in 1964, and the steering column itself could be adjusted for length in a 3in range by using a wrench under the hood.

Beyond was a magnificent set of instruments, speedo and tach surrounded by four smaller gauges and a purposeful clock (with a sweep second hand) set in the central binnacle above the radio. The speedometer read to 160mph and the tach red line started at 5500rpm, or 6500rpm on the 340bhp and 360bhp motors. The '63 dial faces had silvered conical centers from which cranked

A 1963 convertible: the antenna never fully retracted on this model. Bright-finished, coned instruments and a colored plastic rim steering wheel are features of this '63 interior.

orange needles emerged, but the faces were changed to black for '64 – the '63 faces have period charm by day and look tremendous at night.

The radio, although optional, was fitted to all but 967 cars, and probably most of these have had them fitted since. The first radio offered was the AM-only U65 with a signal-seeking powered tuning knob controlled by a Wonderbar lever. An electro-mechanical version of today's digital seek and scan radios, it worked remarkably well. It had two Conelrad markings on the dial, to indicate the civil defence frequencies which would transmit in the event of a national emergency: the cold war was at its height in 1963. This was also the era when the much better quality FM radio transmissions were

beginning and the optional U69 AM/FM was phased in during the year.

Both of these radios required extra shielding from electrical interference from the engine ignition, a function normally fulfilled by the firewall on a steel-bodied car. The shielding was made of stainless steel and neatly fitted with wing nuts to give the engine a very clean appearance. If no radio was fitted, then neither was the shielding. All Corvettes fitted with radios had some form of shielding from 1953 until 1982, by which time radios had improved to the extent that interference was not a problem. Because shielding was inevitably discarded by owners and mechanics over the years, its reproduction and sale has become yet another of those minor Corvette industries.

Transmission..

Between the seats was the gear shift lever. From 1963 to 1967 automatic transmissions accounted for about 10 per cent of sales, stick shifts the remainder. The standard transmission was the Saginaw three-speed, but this iron-cased 'box accounted for only a few hundred sales every year, the automatic or four-speed being worth the extra $200 or so for most buyers.

The option M20 four-speed was at first the same

Instrument panel contrast on '63 and '64 Corvettes: the earlier car's bright-centred dials...

...gave way to a black finish for the new model year, losing some period charm.

aluminum-cased Warner T-10 used in the solid axle cars, but a new and improved 'box replaced it during 1963. This was built at GM's Muncie plant in Indiana – hence the name. The 1964 and later Muncie 'box used a thick chromed shift lever topped by a fat chromed ball, but in 1963 both transmissions used a thin lever with a black plastic ball. Many Corvettes are fitted with Hurst levers: although they were available from new in some GM muscle cars, these were never offered on Corvettes and tend to be fitted as a cheap alternative when the original has worn out. A properly adjusted correct shift not only has a superb feel, but also from 1965 an adjustable throw. Normally used in the easy long-throw position, the rods can be moved to holes closer to the fulcrum of the 1-2 and 3-4 shift levers on the side casing of the 'box, giving a quicker but stiffer shift.

The one-piece rear window that arrived for the '64 Corvette: many owners of the previous year's split-window coupe 'updated' their cars by removing the divider, but today this feature sets the '63 apart as one of the greats. In contrast to the later discs, the drum brakes (below) of '63 and '64 models were trouble-free, if limited in ultimate stopping power.

The Corvette must be unique in having adjustable fast and slow ratio adjustment not only for the gearshift, but also for the clutch lever and steering. The Sting Ray clutch lever has an adjustable upper rod bracket that can be reversed to give short pedal travel, which requires very high driver effort but is ideal, like the fast gear shift, for racing. Similarly, when manual steering is fitted the tie rod ends can be moved from the outer to the inner holes in the steering arm, giving the same faster ratio as the power-assisted car. If this modification is made, the steering toe-in must be re-aligned.

The automatic transmission option M35 was a development of the same basic Powerglide unit that had powered the first Flint-built cars. A two-speed unit only, it would hold low gear to more than 70mph if pressed, depending on the axle ratio. Today many Powerglides feel crude and can be noisy, but if rebuilt carefully they can be very pleasant to drive, and the Powerglide is one of the strongest transmissions ever made. Once dismissed as untrue sports cars, automatics are now particularly sought-after as they are rightly perceived as having been generally better looked after than four-speed cars.

Frame & suspension...............................

The chassis was a steel ladder design with five crossmembers. The rails were made up of two pressed channel sections, overlapped and welded. The transmission crossmember contained twin tubes to accommodate the dual exhaust within its depth to place the car lower to the ground. Using a perimeter chassis rather than the previous X-braced chassis allowed the floor to be dropped between the rails, reducing the height of the car.

Behind the seats the chassis kicked up to accommodate the independent rear suspension, which was a revolutionary concept for a Detroit product at the

As well as the coupe's rear window divider being removed, 1964 saw a change of hubcap (above). A 1964 convertible with factory-fitted knock-off wheels (right): this car has an owner-fitted outside mirror on the passenger side.

time. Perhaps anarchic would be a better word, because Detroit still builds front-engined, rear-drive cars and the majority still have solid axles.

The advantage of an all-wheel independent suspension system is that a single wheel can deal with a bump while the car's weight and smooth progress is handled by the other three. Additionally the deflection of a wheel at one end of a solid axle is inevitably transferred to the whole axle, and therefore to a larger extent the whole car. An independent system also reduces the unsprung weight of the wheel assembly, thereby improving its ability to track over bumps without disturbing the car. Lastly, in straight-line acceleration with a very powerful engine a live axle will be twisted by the engine power, lifting one wheel and causing it to spin. An independent system reduces this effect, and ensures that both wheels have their maximum traction. This made the Corvette a particularly effective car at the drag strip when raced against other production cars. Not surprisingly, once the engine was tuned to drag racing standards and sticky tires were fitted, a weak link was found to be the splined ends of the rear wheel spindles,

Air conditioning and automatic transmission on a '64 car – note the transmission dipstick at bottom left. Air conditioned cars required a specially offset air cleaner to clear the top hose and alternator, which were displaced to the left by the compressor.

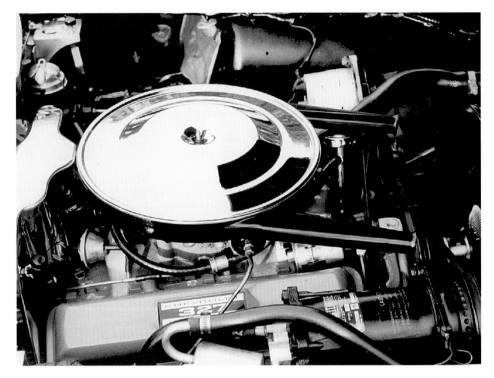

which would twist or break because they had never been designed to handle such torque.

A look at Jaguar's independent rear suspension is interesting because it was the only comparable state-of-the-art system being produced at the time. The Coventry design was superbly engineered with in-board disc brakes, cast aluminum hub carriers, and complex lower links each with four pairs of roller bearings. It was all assembled into a subframe which could be removed from the car, and which formed the top mounting for the four coil-over-shock units.

The Corvette system achieved almost the same geometry, using the drive shaft as the upper link, but with a robust simplicity typical of Detroit. Where the Jaguar has four coil springs, the 'Vette has a single transverse leaf like a Model T Ford. Where the British product has a superb multi-bearing lower link fabricated from five separate pieces and fitted with more than 50 bearings, spacers, seals, washers and nuts, the American cars uses a simple steel rod with a rubber bush at either end. The two systems achieve broadly the same effect, but the Corvette's must have cost less than half the Jaguar's. One wonders who laughed the most – Jaguar's engineers or GM's accountants?

A great deal of energy was expended by the Corvette engineers to make the car handle properly. Zora Arkus-Duntov had established that weight distribution of 49/51

in favor of the rear wheels was the ideal, and the independent rear suspension was comparable to racing car standards of the time. Duntov knew that his new model would be used for racing, and that racing sells cars. He also had to impress the editors and testers of *Car & Driver* and *Road & Track* magazines, whose approval could be a very great influence on sales success. Both of these publications espoused the romance and driver appeal of imported sports cars over any domestic product, so a favorable verdict from them in October 1962 would be doubly effective – they loved it.

The 1964 Sting Ray ....

So strong was demand that the St Louis plant alone could not produce enough Sting Rays. While annual production had never exceeded 10,000 cars until 1960, now the new '63 was about to exceed 20,000 and sales were set to continue improving every year for the next four. Anticipating the demand, Chevrolet contracted the A.O.Smith Company of Ionia, Michigan, to produce additional body units complete with paint and trim. These were to be shipped by railroad to St Louis, where they joined the bodies already made there on the production line as they were about to be united with the chassis. This arrangement started in January 1964 and soon nearly half of Corvette bodies were made in Ionia.

The big change for 1964 was the abandonment of the centre rail that divided the coupe's back window. Bill Mitchell's wish had prevailed for one year, but public opinion forced the change. Now it is a Corvette icon, and we realize that Mitchell was right all along. The cones in the instruments also became matt black, bright metal trim disappeared from the hood and the hubcaps were updated, but otherwise the car was too good to change. Also available after a year's delay were the P48 cast aluminum knock-off wheels, which came as a set of five with a lead hammer to remove them.

Success

Very few cars are so stunning that years later they can still prompt grown men – and women – to debate where they first saw the car, either in print or for real. How much more fun to remember this than where you were when Jack Kennedy was assassinated. The Jaguar XKE was one such landmark design and the first Mustang was another, but the 1963 Corvette was the greatest. A styling *tour de force*, it was a shape conceived for the experimental Q-Corvette of 1957, reworked as a body for Bill Mitchell's own Sting Ray racer of 1959, and then honed for a production car launch in fall 1962.

No matter how good the engine, how brilliant the suspension or even how smooth the ride, an expensive car will never be a real success unless it is wrapped in a beautiful body. In its production form, the Sting Ray was made to look sensational in four formats: convertible with top up, hard-top on, open convertible and, perhaps best of all, split-window coupe.

Beautiful designs in any artistic field tend to be either the work of a single genius or a massive effort by a team of talented people all working towards a common goal. Modern production cars generally, and all GM cars, are designed by the second method. No manufactured artefact contains more man hours of pure design effort than a modern car. Airplanes have more electrical and engineering design input, but they are not styled to please the eye to the same extent. Particularly in the 1960s it could safely be said that the most carefully designed object that an American would see during a normal day would not be a building or a work of art, but an automobile.

Since first seeing Mickey Thompson's 1963 Z06 split-window coupe in *Hot Rod* magazine at the age of 16, I have always thought this the most beautiful of cars. I was fortunate to be able to buy a '66 convertible of my own seven years later, and have always had a Corvette since

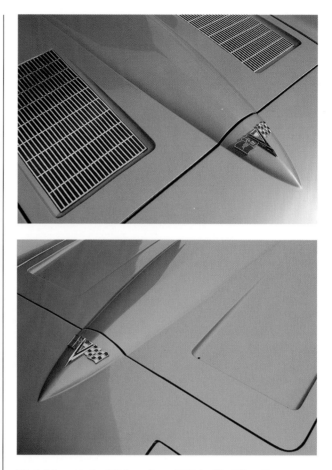

Metal inserts in '63 hood aped the functional, lift-reducing vents in

Mitchell's Sting Ray racer (top), but were discarded for '64 (above).

then. I have been even more fortunate to interview at different times the engineer and honorary father of the Corvette, Zora Arkus-Duntov, and the two great designers, Larry Shinoda and the legendary Bill Mitchell. All three would love to claim the Sting Ray entirely as his own, but each was quick to acknowledge the design as the work of a team.

Chevrolet management knew that they had produced a winner, and all they had to do was to keep making the car and taking the money. Their extraordinary achievement seen with over 30 years of hindsight was to ensure that no-one was allowed to spoil it. Chevrolet's marketing men undoubtedly would have loved to have 'done a Ford'. They could have stretched the wheelbase to incorporate rear seats (a design study was actually prepared for this), changed the body construction to steel, produced 100,000 a year for three years, flooded the market, alienated the sports car buyers, and killed the

Windshield pillars were covered by stainless steel moldings in 1963 (top), **but not in '64 (above). Note how the top of the door cuts into the roof.**

Dummy rear pillar vents on '63 cars (top) were replaced by functional **ones for '64 (above) in order to improve rear ventilation.**

Corvette in five years. Ford did just this with first the Thunderbird and then the Mustang.

Jaguar did an even worse job with the XKE. The company had brilliantly brought its fabulous two-seater to the market more than a year before the Sting Ray, and sold it in exactly the same coupe, convertible and hard-top range, with the advantage of disc brakes and a stiffer body structure than the Corvette. But Jaguar initially failed to address the XKE's shortcomings in the US market, where nearly all were sold. All the XKE needed was the options of power steering, automatic transmission and air conditioning to make the coupe bearable to drive in summer, but Jaguar took a fatal eight years to introduce these. Instead the company did a Ford and offered the car as a four-seater, destroying the sleek, feline shape that made the car into a Corvette competitor in the first place, and diluting the pure two-seater image. Unwilling or unable to re-engineer the car to meet the

federal emissions and crash regulations in its major market, the XKE faded away after 14 years.

The AC Cobra, powered by the Ford 289 V8, was a direct rival to the Corvette convertible and was to compete head to head in competition for years, but as a hand-made car built in very small numbers it did not represent a true alternative. During this period Chevrolet built more Corvettes in a fortnight than the total all-time production of Cobras…

The major mass-produced competitor to the Corvette has always been the Porsche 911. It was introduced two years later than the Sting Ray and followed a successful run by its predecessor, the little 356, which was as old as the solid axle Corvette. But the Porsche was more an alternative than a competitor. With its rear-mounted, rev-happy, air-cooled flat-six and superb detail design, the Porsche generally matched the Corvette in performance, and was considerably better made without

being much more expensive. But the cars are so different that they attract entirely different kinds of drivers. There was hardly any crossover between the two marques then, and the same is true today.

Apart from Porsche and Jaguar, the other cars competing for the attention of the new sports car buyer were all much more expensive imports such as the 250GT V12 Ferraris, the fuel-injected 2.3-liter Mercedes-Benz 230SL convertible and the Aston Martin DB4. Of course, these models were themselves challenged in the market by the much cheaper Corvette.

Among the cheaper imported sports cars, the straight-six 3-liter Austin-Healey 3000 most closely approached the Sting Ray's performance, but it still drove like a stiff straight axle car from a superseded era. The MGB with only 1800cc did not pretend to compete, but interestingly had more legroom for tall drivers. One car that was a true mini Corvette was the Daimler Dart.

Original Chevrolet views of a 1964 convertible. So many Corvettes were fitted with custom wheels that it is now rare to see original hubcaps.

Made by a subsidiary of Jaguar, it had a fiberglass body, ladder frame and a 2.5-liter V8, but it was not a success.

Not only did the appearance of the Sting Ray appeal to a broad range of customers from racers to housewives, but its wide range of options could adjust the character of the car to suit them. Herein lies one of the keys to its success. There is a huge gulf between a racer's ideal Z06 four-speed fuel-injected coupe with heater delete, and a boulevard-cruising, air conditioned powerglide automatic convertible with two tops, leather seats, AM/FM, power steering and power brakes. Yet both of these cars could be ordered from the same dealer for less than $5450, with delivery in 60 days. Better still, both cars could be serviced by any Chevy dealer anywhere.

BUILDING THE CORVETTE

Scene from the Corvette assembly line at St Louis. A car travelled down the line on a body truck running on rails. Here a split-window coupe receives its gas tank emblem.

The Chevrolet plant at St Louis, Missouri, began assembling Corvettes on Monday 28 December 1953, taking over production from the Flint, Michigan, plant where the first 300 cars had been assembled.

Assembly, not manufacture, was the process undertaken. Almost nothing was made at St Louis from steel strip, bar or tube, nor was anything drilled, turned or milled there. Every component came in by truck or railroad from other GM plants or outside suppliers. GM has long worked in this very specialized way, with full-size Chevrolets being assembled in plants across the nation to exactly the same specification. The Corvette has always been assembled at a single location, because by comparison it is a much lower volume car.

All design, engineering evaluation and prototype construction was done at the GM Tech Center at Warren, Michigan, while testing and development happened at the Milford Proving Ground. A fascinating document now universally used by restorers and available for every year in reprint is the *Assembly Instruction Manual*. This is the complete book of instructions to build a Corvette from bumper to bumper, with annotated drawings from the Chevrolet engineering office of every single aspect of constructing the car from the thousands of parts that arrived by truck and rail. Not only are all the part numbers listed, but the exact dimensioned locations, torque figures and types of sealant as well.

The building at St Louis was originally constructed in 1920 as an additional plant to assemble the Chevrolet 490 in the Mid-West. The area later used for Corvette assembly was the Mill building, where the wood for the bodies was processed. This St Louis plant used to be an absorbing place to visit, particularly because the Corvette has always been the world's only mass-produced fiberglass car. The past tense must be used because Corvette

Where Today Meets Tomorrow

GENERAL MOTORS TECHNICAL CENTER

The General Motors Technical Center. Designed chiefly by the Finnish architect Eero Saarinen in 1955 and resembling a modern university campus, this is where all design and engineering work is done. The Styling Dome is in the foreground.

assembly moved to its present purpose-built facility in Bowling Green, Kentucky, in 1981 and all production of other Chevrolet models stopped at the Missouri site in 1987. Today all that remains there is another vacant lot in the Rust Belt.

Today Bowling Green welcomes visitors daily to its bright quality-controlled showpiece, but when I visited the St Louis plant at 3809 Union Boulevard one morning in January 1979 I saw something from a different era. There had been a violent snowstorm the night before and as I was led past the truck assembly area water was dripping through the roof...

Because the frame and running gear were carried through after the end of 1967 production, the line and procedures I saw were virtually unchanged from that date. In 1979 the Corvette was enjoying its peak annual production of 53,807 units – double the level of 15 years earlier – and two nine-hour shifts were being worked to meet demand.

Frames arrived ready painted from A.O.Smith in Milwaukee and started upside-down on the line to allow the suspension, differential and brakes to be installed. It was then flipped over for the exhaust, gas tank, fuel and brake lines to be fitted. The Vehicle Identification Number (VIN) was then stamped at the center and rear of the left frame rail.

The engine arrived ready assembled from Flint if it were a small block, or Tonawanda, New York, for big blocks. These came with the engine number and letter code already stamped on the right-hand mating face of

the cylinder block, and indicated the engine plant, date, horsepower and transmission option. When the appropriate transmission had been bolted into place, the engine and 'box were both stamped with the year of the car and the last six figures of the chassis number. These are the all-important matching numbers which are fully explained and listed in Michael Antonick's indispensible *Corvette Black Book*. The power unit was then dropped into position and the exhausts secured.

Meanwhile the much more time-consuming operation of making the body began with the welding together of the steel 'birdcage' which gave the separate fiberglass body its structural strength. This was painted and fixed to the main underbody panel, and then the whole assembly started down the line on a body truck.

It is always a source of pride to the enthusiastic Corvette owner that admirers invariably need to be convinced that the body is indeed fiberglass. The sceptic will often put his face close to the fender, look along it and exclaim that there are no ripples. Until recently, almost all fiberglass cars except the Corvette were made by the 'boat-building' method, whereby layers of matting are laid into a female mold using a paintbrush to apply the resin. The internal finish with this method is always rough and, at worst, hairy.

By contrast, the Corvette's panels have always been made in a two-stage process, resulting in fiberglass of great strength and with a unique finished surface on both sides. First, resin-coated, chopped fiber was sprayed onto a wire mesh screen and held in place during thickness

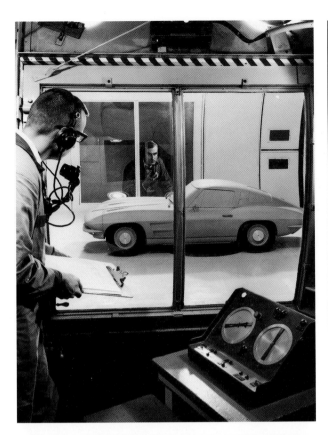

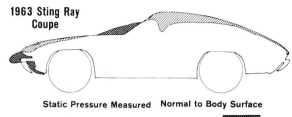

1963 Sting Ray Coupe

Static Pressure Measured   Normal to Body Surface

p.s.i.	0 .08 .16 — 60 mph	Positive
	0 .02 .04 — 30 mph	Negative

Checking aerodynamic performance on a model in the Cal Tech wind tunnel (left). Wind tunnel test results (above). Why does your Sting Ray feel unstable at 125mph? Just look at all that negative pressure trying to lift the car into the air. Basic suspension geometry (below left). Fitting 70- profile radial tires and increasing steering caster to 3.5 degrees works wonders. The fiberglass panels of a 1963 convertible body with a coupe in the background (below). All Corvette panels are formed between matched molds to give a smooth finish on both sides.

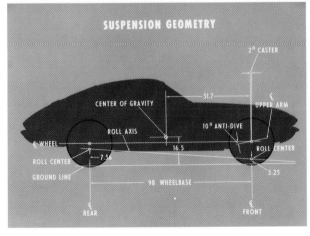

SUSPENSION GEOMETRY

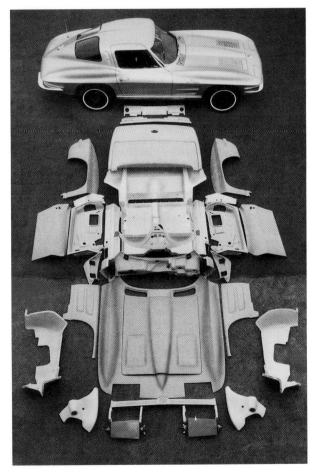

build-up by suction created by fans on the far side of the screen. The semi-cured panel was then placed onto one of a pair of matched dies in a giant press, resin and hardener carefully hand-poured over the still absorbent panel, the press closed and the dies heated until the resin was fully cured. The panel was then removed, checked and the edges trimmed. This process was originally developed for the first Corvette by the Molded Fiberglass Body Company of Ashtabula, Ohio, which was still

Body was fully painted and partly trimmed prior to body drop (left). The 1963 Corvettes were the first to display a paint code, allowing an owner today to find out what color his car was originally painted. The 'birdcage' (below) makes the coupe 90 per cent stiffer in torsion than the convertible, which uses a cut-down version.

making the majority of the panels in 1963.

The body was built up panel by panel, some directly onto the underbody already on the body truck, and others – such as the doors – in the body shop as sub-assemblies. To fix the panels together, they had to scuffed with a grinder to ensure adhesion. Large paper cones were filled with a two-pack bond material, the end of the cone snipped off, and the bond, which became very hot as it started to cure, was applied as though icing a cake. The panels were held in jigs to provide a perfect fit.

Where adjacent panels, such as the upper and lower fenders, had to be butt-jointed, they were backed by a fiberglass bonding strip some 2in wide. The join was then ground and filled. The sight and smell of all this hot and sometimes dusty activity was inspiring, a beautiful body emerging from among the spent bond cones and creeping down the line through endless sanding and smoothing operations on a body truck caked with filler.

Much to my surprise, I was walked straight into the paint booth to stand beside the operators who were painting the cars. Fans in the ceiling were blowing in filtered air, which was sucked out through a floor grid with running water below. A row of spray guns waited on both walls, each loaded with a different color. After ten minutes in the booth, there was no trace of overspray on my glasses…

After painting, the bodies went through a paint reflow oven and arrived at the trim line for all the other components to be fitted up. This began with mounting

the locks and latches for the doors and hood, followed by all glass, lamps, wiring, rear carpets, radiator and battery. The bolts securing the body to the body truck were then removed and the body lifted prior to a full electrical check. I saw the extraordinary sight of a complete instrument panel, console assembly and wiring harness removed, diagnosed, repaired and replaced on the line by three workers in as many minutes – this would take hours for a modern restorer.

At this point it must be reiterated that from 1964 to 1967 approximately half of all Corvette bodies were made at another plant in Ionia, Michigan, by the A.O.Smith Company. Whether this was due to a perceived lack of capacity at St Louis or the first stage of a move of the whole production process back to Michigan

Trimmed '63 coupe body is lowered onto its chassis (right). Between 1964-67, fully-finished A.O.Smith bodies sent by railroad from Ionia, Michigan, were introduced to the line at this point. Final polishing of a finished car (below).

has never been fully explained – but after 1968 all bodies were made in St Louis and production doubled. The A.O.Smith bodies are often said to have been better built, and are identified by an A rather than S prefix on the body number plate on the reinforcement under the glovebox. They arrived fully trimmed on triple-deck railcars and were stored in the basement at St Louis. When required they were lifted onto the line immediately prior to the body drop.

In the final assembly stage, the body was lowered onto the chassis, shimmed and bolted into place, and the bumpers, steering column and wheels and tires installed – the car could now roll on its own wheels. A roadster would now be fitted with its top. The near-complete car was then pulled over the chassis pit where the rear lower

panel and exhaust tips were installed, and parking brake and battery cables connected. Fuel and coolant were added and the engine started for the first time. The driver sat on a stool while the car was tested on rollers and then the car was driven to the water test area, where high-pressure jets tested the car for leaks. I have since been told that during the 1963-67 period some of the jets were permanently blanked off because the convertible could never pass this test…

All bodies were polished and imperfections rectified on the paint repair line, before proceeding to the final trim line where the front carpets, seats, door panels, windshield wipers, seat belts and door sills were fitted. The finished Corvette Sting Ray was given a final coat of shipping wax before being driven outside to await delivery to one of over 6000 Chevrolet dealers.

At the end of this unforgettable tour I was asked how things were at GM's British Vauxhall factory. My reply that I had never been there caused some consternation. Apparently at the time of my visit no outsiders were allowed to see the St Louis plant, and GM Overseas had mistakenly assumed I was an employee when they organized my half-day tour!

A few weeks later rumors started that Corvette assembly was to be moved to a purpose built-facility, away from this decrepit but historic site bordering Natural Bridge Road. So it turned out, and 30 months later the last Corvette to be made in Missouri was driven out into the shipping yard.

BIG BLOCKS AND BIG BRAKES

The first 12 years of Corvette production had seen the power output of the engines more than double. The first 1953 cars were introduced with the straight-six engine which had yielded just 150bhp, but by 1964 the engines were V8s ranging from the 250bhp base version to the optional 375bhp fuel-injected L84. Maximum speed had risen from 107mph for the 1953 model with automatic to 142mph for the '64 fuelie.

Corvettes had become heavier too, the '64 weighing 300lb more than the '53. The independent rear suspension chassis of 1963 could handle the extra power, but needed brakes to match. And so for the 1965 model year the Corvette at last received the brakes it deserved.

GM publicity shot for 1965 fuel-injected coupe, its body looking low by the standards of most modern restored cars.

GM Photographic often loaded cars with weights or hooked them down to cleats in the ground – but this one may be 'honest'.

British Jaguar cars had been the first to use four-wheel disc brakes in sports car racing, with outstanding results, and had followed through into production by fitting them as original equipment on the XK150 in 1957. This model sold outstandingly well in the US, maximising on the association with Jaguar's racing success. When the new shape 1963 Corvette came out eight years later in

A 1965 fuel-injected coupe in Ermine White. Four-wheel disc brakes, this one with the adaptor for a knock-off wheel, were new for '65.

two body styles, it had a specification to compete with the cream of the world's sports and grand touring cars in every area except for brakes. At the time it seemed to be an extraordinary omission. Both in Europe and America, drivers went harder and faster, there being fewer divided highways and freeways and effectively no speed limits on the open road. Drum brakes have always suffered from a fundamental problem when they are used hard and become hot. They cannot dissipate heat fast enough into

The four-wheel disc braking system was extremely powerful, with ventilated rotors all round. A dual-circuit master cylinder was introduced for 1966.

the airstream and so the drums expand and retreat from the shoes, leading to brake fade, a soft pedal and ultimately no braking.

Chevrolet's problem was that it had to develop its own discs and calipers. The Corvette was too fast and heavy to buy in the existing Girling or Dunlop systems used by European competitors. Instead Chevrolet commissioned the Delco Moraine division of GM to design and produce a system capable of handling the Corvette's power and speed. The resulting design was effective enough to be used for the next 18 years of production and powerful enough to be ideal for racing, yet so fundamentally flawed that it would spawn an entire industry involved in the remanufacture of the calipers.

The discs were radially ventilated and of 11.75in diameter. Although visually identical front and rear, they were unfortunately not interchangeable. A drum using conventional shoes was incorporated into the rear disc to serve as a cable-operated parking brake, with adjustment through an access hole in the disc onto a star wheel. The calipers were heavy iron castings, rigidly mounted with two pistons each side, 1⅞in front and 1⅜in rear, to achieve the correct front to rear balance. Pistons were anodized aluminum and were fitted with hard plastic insulators at the pad end to prevent fluid boil. Although until this time conventional wisdom held that disc brakes always needed a vacuum-operated power brake booster, this was an option that was taken up by only 15 per cent of 1965 buyers. Chevrolet had decided that the new

brake system had to operate unboosted in order to save cost and meet the car's price target.

In designing this new brake system to work unboosted, the brake pads had to be in constant rubbing contact with the rotors, to allow sufficient mechanical advantage at the pedal without excessive travel. While this arrangement improved wet-weather performance by continuously drying the contact areas, it increased friction and therefore fuel consumption. When gasoline was 10 cents a gallon this was of little significance, but nowadays it can be a consideration in favor of the 1963-64 cars. To anyone lucky enough to be able to drive regularly a range of mid-period Sting Rays, the lack of rolling resistance in the drum-braked cars is quite striking. On my own commute to work there is a two-mile stretch of country road which slopes gently downhill. Pre-1965 or post-1984 Corvettes – or my bicycle! – will accelerate when coasting, but 1965-82 models slow almost to a stop. It must also be said that with the improvement in roads and the imposition of speed limits over 30 years, we all now use our brakes much less than we used to.

The Corvette's disc brakes are so incredibly powerful and effective that any 1965-82 car may almost be considered overbraked, and yet in damp climates the brakes were failing completely as little as five years into a car's life. The blame for this unfortunate situation was not entirely Chevrolet's, but really lay with successive owners who failed to change the brake fluid annually in accordance with good practice. The reaction of cast iron to moisture is the fundamental cause of the Corvette caliper problem. Conventional Glycol-based DOT3 brake fluid is hygroscopic – it absorbs water from the atmosphere. If brake fluid is not changed annually the accumulated moisture will rust the polished cast iron bore surfaces, causing pitting on the sealing surface that no amount of polishing or honing will remove without leaving the bore too large. Thankfully the problem was eventually solved by fitting post-1984 Corvettes with aluminum calipers.

Very often this caliper problem will manifest itself as a loss of pedal pressure and braking efficiency, but with no fluid leakage at all around the calipers – indeed these will often appear completely dry externally. This symptom can also be accompanied by an apparent rise in the level of fluid in the master cylinder. The explanation for this is that the caliper bores have deteriorated to the extent that they will allow air to be sucked past the piston seals on the return stroke of the brake pedal, while still retaining the fluid – which of course is thicker than air. As air accumulates in the calipers, so the pedal softens and the fluid level rises.

The fact that the pads are in constant contact with the discs has one additional and unfortunate consequence when the bores of the calipers have rusted and allowed air past them. Because the discs cannot run perfectly true, and the wheel bearings must have some free play, the disc will constantly move the pads – and therefore the pistons in and out of the bores – whenever the car is running. The unsuspecting buyer of a Corvette which apparently has perfect brakes can therefore drive 100 miles home on the freeway, only to find himself pushing the brake pedal through the floor and sailing out of control through the first traffic light in his home town...

Fortunately this problem has an easy solution involving only two or three hours' labor. The stainless steel sleeved caliper was invented and perfected in the mid-1970s. The bores are drilled out oversize and stainless steel sleeves inserted and polished. A number of manufacturers now offer these as exchange units fully assembled with new

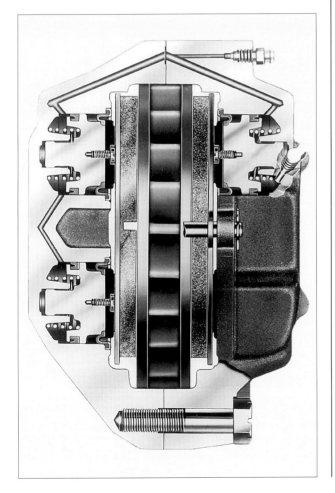

The Corvette brake caliper (left). This is the 1965-66 type, the pistons having insulators and guides. The majority of Sting Rays probably now have after-market stainless steel sleeved calipers, a permanent solution to the corrosion problems which afflict the bores of the original cast iron units. The 1964-66 knock-off aluminum wheel (above) looked great but weighed more than the stock steel wheel and trim.

A 1965 coupe interior (left), with flat-faced instruments and electric windows. Instead of having four tail lights (below), the inner pair could be ordered as back-up lamps (bottom), operated by a switch on the transmission – this feature became standard for 1966.

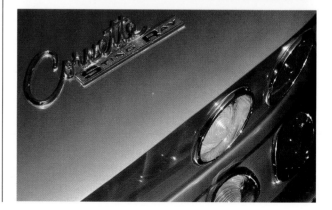

seals and pistons ready to bolt on. As always, owners with mechanical aptitude and access to machining facilities attempt to modify their own calipers, often with poor results. Sometimes they leak fluid down the back of the sleeve, or worse the sleeve pops out during a hard stop. The good manufacturers clearly stamp their logo and serial number on their calipers and these are superb products.

The parking brake mechanism has always suffered from being hidden inside its own drum, accessible only by removing the brake caliper and drilling out the soft rivets which retain it to the drive flange. Again the companies remanufacturing brakes have devised their own solution, reproducing all the parking brake components in stainless steel. Note that this brake is referred to as a parking brake and not an emergency brake. Since this drum's diameter is just 6½in, the Corvette owner is better advised to steer round his emergency than attempt to stop using this brake!

For the 1965 model year only, drum brakes were offered as an option in place of the new discs, but only 316 owners opted to save themselves $64.50 this way. Thirty years later, such a brake delete car would be a highly prized and valuable find, for its scarcity alone...

The big-block arrives ....

The 1965 model year also marked the beginning of the Corvette's 10-year flirtation with the Mark IV or big-block engine. Taking advantage of the improved brakes

The 1965 model year was the last for fuel injection, which was wiped away by demand for the cheaper big-block. Unique on a mass-produced sports car, injection had been an option since 1957.

The engine bay of 1965 396cu in big-block with 425bhp.

to install this heavier and much more powerful engine, Chevrolet offered the 396cu in 425bhp version from March 1965, halfway through the model year. Whether fitting the big-block engine into the Corvette was ever a good idea is still open to conjecture. If your previous car was a Pontiac GTO and your favorite sport was drag racing, suddenly in 1965 Corvette was your kind of car. But if you had just moved up from a Jaguar XKE and liked SCCA circuit racing, you were unlikely to have your salesman check the L78 box on the order form.

The Chevy big-block engine was a sensation when it was introduced. Broadly based on the 427cu in version of the Mark II or 'W' engine that had been an option for full-size Chevrolets since 1958 and was famous as the 409, the Mark IV sported very special cylinder heads. Chevrolet V8s have always used studs rather than shafts to mount their rockers. On the small-block these were arranged in a straight line and on the 'W' they were offset to accommodate larger valves, but on the Mark IV the studs and valves were cleverly inclined to improve combustion chamber and port shape. With the enormous valve covers, springs and rockers removed, studs and valve stems stick up at all angles, hence the nickname 'Porcupine' for the heads.

The big-block was easy to install into the '65 Corvette. The engine mounting and bellhousing bolt patterns were identical, the main modification required being a different hood to accommodate the taller motor. This new panel was styled to incorporate a pair of functional chromed grilles and was used only on cars fitted with the new motor. Each upper fender also displayed a '396 Turbo-Jet' emblem: Turbo-Jet was the marketing department's new name for the Mark IV family of engines, the small-block series being called

Turbo-Fire. While such names may be synonymous with power and speed to the refrigerator salesmen who constitute the average marketing department, they were sensibly never adopted by enthusiasts in general, who understood the meaning of the word Turbo and at that time associated it with Corvairs and not Corvettes. The new big-block started to be referred to as the 'Rat' and the small-block as the 'Mouse'.

So that it could not be accused of building over-engined cars, GM corporate policy determined that no intermediate-sized model could be fitted with an engine of more than 400cu in. In retrospect, the mid-1960s muscle cars such as the Pontiac GTO were seriously over-powered not only for their size, but more particularly for their solid rear axles, inadequate drum brakes and grip-free belted tires. With its strong disc brakes and effective independent rear suspension, the Corvette was a much safer road car, but for the half-year of 1965 only its big-block was built down to 396cu in (with a 4.09in bore and a 3.76in stroke). The under-hood appearance of the engine was tremendous: the staggered rockers and valves required giant valve covers to hide them, making this engine a far more impressive sight than the Cadillac or Pontiac big-blocks.

During this engine's 10 years of use in Corvettes, displacements of 396, 427 and 454 were produced, the last two introduced respectively for 1966 and 1970. While all are externally identical in appearance except for casting numbers, the 396 and 427 share the same 3.76in

Badging details from 1965. Crossed flags motif on nose (below left) was repeated on the gas filler door (below), which concealed the gas cap beneath – each year of the Sting Ray has a different pattern of filler door.

A 1965 350/350 with air conditioning, its air cleaner removed to show the aluminum intake manifold and Holley 4150 carburetor.

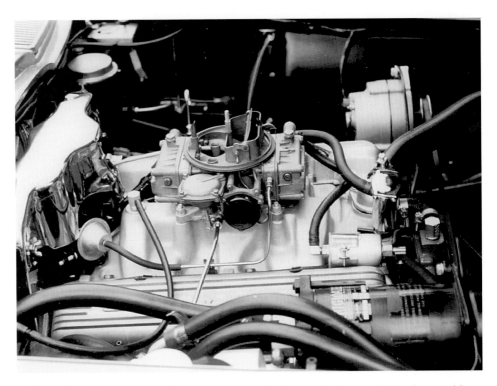

stroke crankshaft, and the 427 and 454 share the same 4.25in bore block. The L78 396 engine was rated at 425bhp at 6400rpm using 11.0:1 compression pistons, solid lifters and a Holley four-barrel carburetor. Even more impressive was its 415lb ft of torque at 4000rpm, with massive torque available right through the power band, even down to idle.

No-one can forget their first drive in a big-block Corvette. Most impressive is the performance in third and fourth gears. Once you have shifted up there is no need to downshift for passing or climbing hills – just press that right foot down and the distance rushes towards you. There is so much torque that on a steep hill, for which you would have to shift down a gear in any other car, the big-block climbs and accelerates in top. So much power brings with it some disadvantages too. While the small-block is always smooth even when pressed hard, the big-block is a shaker when wound up. The extra weight of the bigger crank and the reciprocating rods and pistons is multiplied many times when the engine is revving, and this vibrates the car in a particular way which some will love but others will find infuriating on a long journey, particularly in a coupe. Of course, exactly the same criticism can be levelled at Harley Davidsons, and this does not diminish their appeal at all…

The extra 150lb weight of the big-block redistributed the Corvette's balance so that 51 per cent of the weight was now over the front axle, the car feeling less nimble as a consequence. Heavier front coil springs compensated for the extra weight, while a rear sway bar was added to improve control and was subsequently fitted to all Corvette big-blocks.

Externally, the 1965 car was given three functional vertical front fender louvers in place of the previous closed horizontal vents. The hood used with the small-

Underside of the deck lid with soft-top stowed. With practice the driver can put the top down without having to leave the seat…

The Mark IV big-block motor was first offered in the Corvette in March 1965 as a 425bhp 396, the engine fitted to this sparkling convertible

(facing page). A 1966 427 convertible with soft-top raised smokes its tires during performance figuring for *Road & Track* magazine.

block lost its recesses, and with them the unsightly holes required to drain away rain water. Why should such a pure and beautifully shaped car as the Corvette have required these hood recesses in the first place? The '65 certainly looked better without them, but they represented a link with the original manifestation of the shape in the Sting Ray racer, and it is probable that Mitchell held out for them to be retained. There is another factor to consider: although not subject to the same annual restyles as other GM passenger cars, the Corvette had to look different each year and having those depressed hood grilles available to lose in two stages was useful. The crossed-flag emblems and the ornate gas filler lid were updated to a more modern style.

An outstanding new option finally made its way into production after use on almost all of the dream cars and racing prototypes. Side exhausts were offered for $134.50 in combination with a plain rear lower panel with no

tailpipe outlets. Supplied with 2in or 2½in pipes as required for small-block or big-block engines, they exited the standard cast iron manifolds and swept out behind the front wheels, where they entered the pinched pipe section that pretended to be a muffler. This was in turn covered with a slotted and polished cover which went some way toward protecting the legs from burns, but on a hot day after a fast run a warning to your passenger becomes second nature to the side-pipe driver, particularly if those legs are bare and female. The sound of side pipes is heaven on short drives, but can turn into hell on longer ones.

In the cockpit the instruments and time clock lost their conical faces and cranked needles, to be replaced by plain black but very attractive flat faces. Unfortunately, the odometer gears were always a weak point, often failing well before 70,000 miles had been reached. The impulse-wound Borg clock also failed, generally through lack of regular lubrication, and most restorers now convert these to a quartz movement. As with every year, the control knobs and lighter were also restyled.

The seats were changed to make them more comfortable and improved in appearance by using large plain panels, in vinyl or optional leather, rather than the

GM publicity picture of a pre-production 1966 coupe (above), with side emblems missing. Side-mounted exhausts (left), optional between 1965-67, used a single pipe to the stock cast manifold, and were never quiet.

Big-block cars had a special hood with a grille each side (below) to accommodate the taller and heavier motor. A 1966 big-block roadster, painted Rally Red and with side-mounted exhaust (facing page).

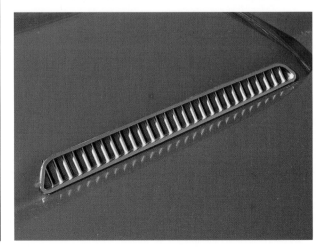

multiple pleats of previous years. Carpet fit was improved and simplified by factory press molding prior to installation. In this process, a thermoset compound was incorporated into the backing of the loop-pile carpet so that one piece of carpet would fit each floor well. Previously the wells were carpeted with a number of pieces each with bound edges.

Door panels also were changed completely for 1965. The preceding year's door panels had vinyl fabric and trim glued and stapled over a dense board, the door armrest being screwed on separately. Now the door panels were hard foam-filled composites, formed onto a molded fiberboard backing and finished in grained vinyl on the face to incorporate a molded armrest and stainless trims. Like so many technical advances, these were great panels from the perspective of GM, whose only interest was in satisfying the first owner, but they were not so good for subsequent owners because they deteriorated fast. The vinyl was stretched thin over the armrest sections and cracked, while the fiberboard backing panels curled and failed as they absorbed moisture. This type of construction was used in Corvettes for a further 12 years and in many GM cars worldwide over the same period.

For many years owners could do nothing to repair them, but as with all things Corvette the after-market industry was waiting to help, and these panels are now available in superb reproductions built on a stout plastic rather than fiberboard backing, and in all the correct colors.

The 1965 model year was the last in which Rochester fuel injection was offered. It had become almost an anachronism in the new muscle car era where cubic inches spoke loudest. The new big-block had more power and much more torque for only half the extra cost. Even though it was only introduced for the second half of the year, more than 2000 big-blocks were sold against only 771 fuelies. The time for multi-port fuel injection, with its fuel economy and driveability, had passed, but it would return as the Corvette's saviour in 1985.

Into 1966 . . . .

More power and more cubic inches was the big theme for 1966, with the 396 gaining a bigger bore to become a 427 – a full 7 liters. Zora Arkus-Duntov denied that this was to increase power: "Cast iron is very heavy, and by removing 30cu in of it we have made a significant

A 1966 coupe with back-up lamps on (left): this one has the small-block motor and stock wheels, and the lack of rear pillar vents is a feature new for '66. Fine angle of a '66 427 convertible (below): for 1966 the big-block was enlarged to a full 7 litres, giving a regular 390bhp or 425bhp for the solid-lifter version. GM publicity views of a 1966 427 with optional hard-top in position (facing page). This could be ordered either as a no-cost alternative to the soft-top or a $231.75 extra.

reduction in weight". There was now a choice of big-blocks: the L36 with 10.25:1 compression, hydraulic lifters and two-bolt main bearing caps had 390bhp, while the L72 with 11.0:1 compression, solid lifters and four-bolt caps produced 425bhp.

The sweet-running Carter carbureted 250bhp 327, which had been the base engine since the upgrade from 283cu in 1962, was dropped, so that a 300bhp now became the standard motor, fuelled by a Holley.

All 1966 Corvettes used Holley four-barrel carburetors. Contrary to popular opinion, I maintain that this was a retrograde step. The problem with the Holley four-barrel is that it was designed primarily for drag racing. When used for circuit racing, centrifugal force during hard cornering piles the fuel to the outside of the float bowls and starves the jets. But at the drag strip, one can change these jets between runs, so easily do the float bowls remove. This quick-change facility is the source of

the Holley problem: the carburetor is split vertically so that it has no more chance of remaining leak-free than does a Triumph twin motorcycle engine with its similarly vertically-split crankcase. When it becomes hot in normal road use the carburetor body also tends to distort, resulting in air leaks. Within two years Holleys were being phased out in favor of the horizontally-split GM Rochester four-barrel in all except high-performance engines, where they hung on until 1972.

Other changes for 1966 were minor: the optional back-up lamps became standard, the Corvette script was updated to an upright style, and the seats gained more pleats. The hubcaps of the standard wheels were changed again and the center cones of the knock-off wheels were given a satin finish.

The 1966 model year Sting Ray was scheduled to be the last of this shape, to be replaced by the new model, but this was not to happen quite yet…

RACING THE CORVETTE

As soon as the V8 motor had replaced the old six-cylinder, it became inevitable that the Corvette would be raced. Not only was the car now much more powerful, but the short-stroke engine also had the potential to be tuned: it was at the beginning, not the end, of its development life.

For the privateer, the car had an excellent power to weight ratio, and a light, high-revving, big engine placed well behind the front axle in a 2800lb body had to make a great deal of sense. For the factory, racing the Corvette offered Chevrolet not only the immediate prospect of favorable column inches, but the possibility of a complete change of image away from the days of the VIP Six.

Zora Arkus-Duntov was Chevrolet's own tame racer – he even drove a Porsche at the 1953 Le Mans while a

John Fitch at Daytona Beach, Florida, in 1956. Plexiglass headlamp fairings, aero windshield and tail fin are gestures towards drag reduction.

Chevrolet employee. Duntov knew that racing could hold the key to the Corvette's future credibility, but with experience of thousands of test miles he also knew that the handling, and in particular the brakes, would be weaknesses on the track. Realising that the Corvette's strongest card was its powerful engine and low wind resistance, he initially hatched a plan to go record-breaking rather than racing, at the annual Daytona Speed Week in Florida.

After extensive testing at the Mesa, Arizona, GM research facility, Duntov took his test 'mule' onto the

Three ages of Corvette racing derivatives: landmark Sting Ray racer (foreground) with SR-2 of 1957 and Grand Sport no. 003 from 1963.

sandy foreshore at Daytona Beach, Florida, and set a two-way average speed of 150.58mph in January 1956. For Speed Week in February he arranged for two more cars, 1956 models, to be fitted with his special long-duration camshaft, and these were driven by well-known sports car driver John Fitch (who had co-driven the Cunningham which finished third at Le Mans in 1953) and famous aerobatic stunt flyer Betty Skelton.

The history of the Corvette has been recounted many times, and this record run is duly mentioned. But it has always struck me as an extraordinarily brave exploit. All

Corvettes made in the past 10 years can top 150mph and I have driven them at this speed myself a few times when a smooth and empty stretch of unrestricted European freeway has tempted me. I also once nudged 140mph in my old '66 327/350 before backing off in fear of the steering's lightness at this speed. But to sustain 150mph on damp sand, with no roll cage and on snow tires to improve the grip, is surely truly courageous!

The desired publicity followed, and the order was given by Ed Cole to enter the following month's Sebring 12-hour endurance race, with John Fitch organising the four-car team. Two of the four cars finished, limping home, but this was sufficient for advertising agency Campbell Ewald to compose its legendary 'The Real McCoy' advertisement which ran in *Hot Rod* and *Road &*

55

The Corvette SS as it survives today (left) and during race preparation in 1957 (below). It raced only once, at Sebring in 1957, before being withdrawn because of the AMA racing ban.

Track magazines for July 1956. Chevrolet had raced the Corvette and not only survived but was reaping the benefits. Dick Thompson won the amateur Sports Car Club of America Production Class C Championship, and tied for first place overall.

Although a detailed account is beyond the scope of this book, some further pre-1963 racing history is needed to set the scene for the Sting Ray. For the 1957 season, Duntov persuaded management to approve a genuine Corvette sports racing car, to be designed to compete with the Jaguar D-type and Mercedes-Benz 300SLR, and to win at Le Mans. It was called the SS (for Super Sport) and used a fully triangulated space-frame chassis, de Dion rear suspension and the new Corvette fuel injection. It was clothed in the most beautiful special body by Harley Earl's styling staff, and the whole car was finished to the highest show standards.

It appeared at the 1957 Sebring 12 Hours, only just completed and barely run in, but failed to finish through mechanical ailments in spite of valiant efforts by driver John Fitch and an enthusiastic crew. The crowd's response to the SS was fantastic – an American racing car taking on Ferraris, Maseratis and Jaguars. Even better, the two top international Grand Prix drivers of the day and eventual winners, Stirling Moss and Juan Manuel Fangio, both tried the spare 'mule' car during practice sessions and loved it. This 'mule', incidentally, later became the Sting Ray racer.

End of a fruitful racing era for the Corvette, as Black leads Fuller at Sebring in 1962.

A three-car team was entered for the French 24-hour race with some confidence of winning. Ed Cole, who was right behind the project, even proposed developing desmodromic valve gear, which would mechanically close the valves rather than relying on springs, allowing the engine to rev to 9000rpm and produce 400bhp.

Disaster then struck. The big three – GM, Ford and Chrysler – agreed to ban completely all factory participation in any branch of motor sport. Ironically, this had nothing to do with the SS program. Instead, according to Gregory von Dare in his excellent *Corvette Racers*, this was the result of an approach by NASCAR to the big three to reduce their factory support because private entrants were being outclassed. There was little enthusiasm about racing in senior management and the 'anti' faction were happy to support a ban which effectively lasted for seven years, and which colored GM's attitude for much longer. Sports car racing was insignificant compared with NASCAR, but the effect on factory Corvette racing was the same: all work on the SS had to stop. The 1957 Le Mans turned out to be a 1-2-3-4 clean sweep for Jaguar. How competitive might the SS Corvette have been? It would have had more power, but would have lacked the disc brakes which gave the D-type so much superiority over its rivals.

Meanwhile, amateur drivers in SCCA racing found the Corvette to be the answer to their prayers. It was already robust and easily affordable, but Chevrolet then

introduced a program of heavy duty parts that were designed to turn the Corvette into a race car. By ordering your 1960 with RPO (Regular Production Option) 687, you received special front and rear shocks, metallic brake linings with air scoops and cooling fans, and a steel plate with two U-clamps which bolted to the centre steering link and reduced the steering ratio from 21:1 to 16.3:1. With this option you also had to have either the 250bhp or the 290bhp fuelie motor, Positraction differential and a manual gearbox. All this could be yours for under $550, and you could also select the 24-gallon gas tank if you did not mind losing the stowage space for the convertible top which this occupied.

On the track these cars were always spectacular. It has been said that a sports car needs 10 per cent more power than its chassis can handle in order to be fun to drive. By this definition a racing Corvette was the perfect sports car: on the tracks Corvettes invariably cornered tail-out and always thrilled the crowds, the drivers sawing away at their close-set steering wheels in the old-fashioned bent-arm style of their childhood heroes at Indianapolis or the Nürburgring.

The 1963 Sting Ray was a completely new car with only the engine and transmission carried over from the previous model. For the first time it was offered as a fully enclosed car incorporating a steel birdcage which promised far greater torsional stiffness to allow the suspension to work properly, and, no less important,

Ace lensman Bob Tronolone's marvellous Sting Ray racer views of Dick Thompson at Riverside in October 1960. Very few action photographers were shooting color this early...

better roll-over protection. There was a lower center of gravity, and a far better driving position which allowed the possibility of the modern straight-arm style. It was more streamlined, but best of all it looked great – a car the racers wanted to be seen in. The future indeed looked promising.

Also carried over from the previous year was the option of heavy duty parts for competitive use. The new RPO number was Z06, and was based on the 360bhp fuel-injected motor with four-speed transmission and Positraction. Then there was the heavy duty brake package, booster assisted and with scoops directing cooling air onto the backing plates. Suspension was modified with stiffer springs and shocks, and a thicker

Two scenes from the Corvette Sting Ray's race debut at Riverside in the *Los Angeles Times* Grand Prix on 13 October 1962. Bob Bondurant refuels in car 614, while Doug Hooper acknowledges victory in car 119. Hereafter the rival Cobras would prove to be a thorn in the Sting Ray's flesh...

front sway bar. Rear sway bars were not introduced until 1965, and then only on the big-block cars. Initially introduced for coupes only, the package was to include knock-off aluminum wheels and a 36-gallon fuel tank mounted within the rear compartment. The knock-off wheels were never fitted to production cars in 1963 so the Z06 package was changed to exclude these last two items, and extended to the convertible car as well. The

big gas tank option was fitted to a few hundred cars between 1963-67, and there is evidence that not all were used for carrying gasoline. At least one car has been found in the Deep South with the tank disconnected from the engine and a lingering smell of moonshine...

Four of the first Z06 cars were collected from St Louis and driven to California to put some break-in mileage on them before being raced at the *Los Angeles*

Sting Ray action from 1963. Dick Thompson (above) wins at Marlboro, Maryland, while Delmo Johnson and Dave Morgan (left) make a pitlane call during their run to 16th place at Sebring – see the spare tire in the back of the car? George Wintersteen (facing page) winning the GT class of the 1966 Daytona 24 Hours in a Penske-run modified production Corvette.

Times Grand Prix at Riverside, on 13 October 1962. What could be more blissful than to drive four brand-new, factory-prepped, fuel-injected coupes almost the full length of Route 66, in an America innocent of speed limits in the fall of 1962, with High Test 102-octane gas available all the way?

The race was a three-hour enduro for production cars and the Corvette drivers were Bob Bondurant, Dave MacDonald, Jerry Grant and Doug Hooper (the last in a car belonging to hot rodder Mickey Thompson). It could have been reasonably expected that the Corvettes would sweep all before them at their first appearance. They were the fastest production cars driven by the best drivers, but on the day another new car, the AC Cobra, made its first racing appearance and ran rings around the Corvettes before it broke, leaving Hooper to win. He finished at an average speed of 84mph with just one pit stop to add 31 gallons to his big tank. He was thrilled to have won for Chevrolet in the car's maiden race.

The Ford-powered AC Cobra was 1000lb lighter than the Corvette, and competing against it quite unfairly – it was bound to be faster than the Corvette and was. The Cobra grew from a hand-built English sports car that normally ran a 2-liter six-cylinder, until Carroll Shelby had the brilliant idea of shoehorning in the Ford 289 V8 of more than twice the capacity. He had only built three

cars prior to this race, but the Cobra's reputation was made. It instantly became one of the world's fastest production cars and is still a legend today. Whereas the Corvette was still a mass-produced, dual-purpose, luxury personal car which could be taken racing, the Cobra was a racing car which could be used on the road for uncomfortable but fantastically stimulating short trips. There was now a real alternative to the 'Vette in SCCA production racing and the top drivers switched in droves.

One man at Chevrolet would not take this lying down – Zora Arkus-Duntov. He knew the Sting Ray's strengths and limitations as a racing car, and realized that it could only be winner on the track as long as nothing lighter came along, so he had approached the new Chevrolet head, Bunkie Knudsen, before the Sting Ray's launch with a proposal to build a lightweight version. Since it was to be the same car, only lighter, it did not need to be submitted for approval by the GM Engineering Policy Committee, which would surely not have accepted it. Ford was backing the Cobra and making its first moves towards the GT40 that would eventually win Le Mans, so it was reasonable to assume that GM would also loosen up in due course.

The plan was to build 125 units of the new lightweight, to be called the Grand Sport. It was to have the profile and appearance of the coupe version, but with

David and Goliath? Sting Ray passes a Lola on the Daytona banking in 1963 (above). Unknown Corvette driver at Bridgehampton in 1965 chases a Chaparral 2A (left).

the back window divider omitted because Duntov had never liked it, and with the headlamps behind plexiglass covers. The considerable wind resistance of the car was to be compensated by the much lighter body and chassis, and a massively powerful motor.

The perimeter frame with its rear kick-up was ditched in favor of a ladder chassis with two longitudinal tubes of large diameter – a very similar structure to the Cobra's and extremely light at only 160lb. The suspension was all specially fabricated but followed normal Corvette practice with a transverse rear spring. Disc brakes were installed, using British Girling calipers: these were fine for the racer but would have been inadequate to stop the heavier production car, for which discs were still two years away.

The body, made in the engineering department, used ultra-thin fiberglass of just 0.040in thickness. To meet FIA regulations, a trunk lid was installed to access the spare tire, while the fuel filler was in the roof. The car ran a finished interior, complete with stock steering

The ultimate competition Sting Ray. The first of the five Grand Sports under construction, before body modifications began, and finished in white paint.

Grand Sport's independent rear suspension arrangement was shared with the production Corvette.

wheel and a special 200mph speedometer. The Grand Sport weighed under 2000lb – less than the Cobra. An all-aluminum 377cu in engine was built, using Duntov-designed cylinder heads with hemispherical combustion chambers and twin spark plugs. Rochester fuel injection was used with individual ram pipes rather than the standard car's plenum. The new motor tested out at 550bhp at 6400rpm.

The FIA agreed to the car being acceptable in the Grand Touring category of the World Sports Car Championship, subject to 100 being completed by June 1963. The AMA ban which had killed off the SS was now being ignored by two out of three of its original signatories, leaving only GM in place, but in February 1963 the axe fell once again as GM president Ralph Donner reaffirmed the 'no racing' policy.

The GS program was stopped with only five cars half-built. But Chevrolet had no intention of wasting the work already done, and two cars were completed and loaned to Dick Doane and Grady Davis. Powered by

Grand Sports arriving for their *tour de force* at Nassau in December 1963. Conceived in an era of narrow tires, these cars sprouted ugly flares to accommodate newly available wide tires.

conventional 360bhp fuelie motors, the GS made its racing debut at the now-abandoned Marlboro track in Maryland, where Dick Thompson drove the Davis car in the C Modified instead of the GT class for which it had been designed. The first victory came at Watkins Glen, again with Thompson driving, after improved dual-inlet fuel injection had been fitted.

Meanwhile the Cobras carried all before them with ample support from Dearborn, and so the ever-enthusiastic Knudsen fought back once more, breaking all the corporate rules. The Doane and Davis cars were recalled to the Tech Center and together with a third car were specially prepared for an all-out assault on the Cobras at Nassau Speed Week in the Bahamas. The three were fitted with 377cu in aluminum motors with cross-ram manifolds and four Weber carburetors, and sat on ultra-wide low-profile racing tires on Halibrand knock-off wheels, with ugly bodywork extensions to cover them. The cars were sprayed in the metallic blue of the John Mecom Jr racing team from Houston, and would be raced by his drivers Roger Penske, Augie Pabst, Jim Hall, John Cannon and Dick Thompson.

The Grand Sports comprehensively beat the Cobras in both the 112-mile Governor's Cup and the 252-mile Nassau Trophy, and the many Chevrolet engineers who 'by chance' were in Nassau on vacation went home happy. Buoyed by this success, they rebodied the remaining two cars as roadsters with a cut-down windshield to reduce frontal area. These cars were entered in the 1964 Daytona Continental, much of which was run on the high-speed banked tri-oval. Once more GM president Donner stepped in to stop all racing, and this time the Grand Sports had to be destroyed. But once again the enthusiasts stepped in and instead arranged that they be sold off. The cost of developing the five cars must have been phenomenal, but they were sold for a nominal sum to racers who could be trusted to continue to wave the Chevy flag.

Two of the GS coupes were sold to John Mecom Jr, and one to Jim Hall. The latter tells the story that his local Chevy dealer called to tell him that a funny-looking Corvette had arrived on a transporter and would he please come down and pay for it. The invoice said only: 'One Chevrolet Corvette Coupe – no options – list price $4257'! The two roadsters were sold to Penske in 1966.

The five Grand Sports are the most valuable and highly-prized of Corvettes, and all still exist today. They had the misfortune to be stuck with an outdated

Restored Grand Sports in action in modern times. Car 50, seen in the Bahamas (above) and at Laguna Seca (right), is chassis 004, and car 2 is chassis 003.

Dick Thompson's Grand Sport leading pole-winner Augie Pabst's prototype Lola at Nassau in 1963. With its built-in aerodynamic lift and massive power, the GS always looked excessively nose-high under acceleration.

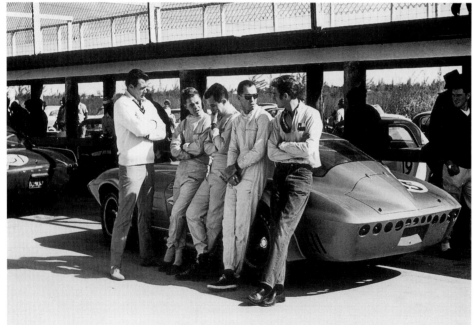

Relaxing at Nassau are, from left, team owner John Mecom Jr with drivers Augie Pabst, Roger Penske, Dick Thompson and Jim Hall.

aerodynamic profile when vast progress was being made by others in this field. While the rest of the racing world was starting to get car noses down toward the ground, the GS always held its nose higher the faster it went.

The Corvette may not have had much luck in beating the Cobra over this period, but it had no problem outnumbering it. The Corvette remained the staple amateur race car: fast, safe, fun, reliable and cheap. There was almost no limit to the performance parts available,

with more choice than for any other engine ever.

The advertising always gave the impression that your 'Vette could take out your date on Saturday night and see you in the winner's circle on Sunday afternoon. But racers are not like this: even when they are not driving into each other or the Armco, they destroy their cars in the pursuit of lightness and speed. The whole interior, gearshift, instruments, bumpers, headlights, wheels and exhaust are jettisoned and the car soon becomes fit for

Two of the Grand Sports were converted to roadster form in April 1964 (above). It was hoped that cutting off the roof would reduce the massive drag. One of the roadsters was sent to an exhibition in 1965 (right), virtually in road trim, and eventually both were sold to Roger Penske.

only a trailer. The body is then cut about for roll cages, fender flares, hood scoops and brake cooling. Fortunately, documented cars that raced almost from new are now valuable and prized in vintage racing, but very few of the Z06 cars have survived.

My first taste of Corvettes racing was heard, not seen. Driving through the Napa Valley on a hot Saturday afternoon, I was suddenly aware of explosions of sound interspersed by squealing noises off somewhere to my right. Driving a little further I found myself at Sears Point circuit with a Corvette race in progress. While smaller cars can be driven round a tight circuit with power on all the way, Corvettes, particularly big-blocks with their excess of power, seem to leap from one corner to the next in a thunderclap of sound, scrabble their way untidily around the bend, and then leap again to the next. It is spectacular and satisfying to watch the ultimate macho sports car in action on the race track.

THE 1967 STING RAY

Corvette Sting Ray Convertible with GM-developed energy-absorbing steering column, padded sun visors and windshield washer standard.

'67 Corvette

Good second hand car.

Go ahead. Match the Corvette Sting Ray against the second hand. Put it through its paces the way you think a car like this one ought to be tried. Then come talk to us about sports cars.

Tell us of another sports car with Corvette's combination of comfort, convenience and pure performance.

Tell us of another sports car you can tailor so exactly to your desires—five engines, three transmissions, axle ratios from here to there and back again. And there are two different models. Mix to suit yourself.

Show us another luxury sports car—even at twice Corvette's price—that can stop a watch the way the Sting Ray can. Go ahead. Tell us. If you can.

CHEVROLET

It seems extraordinary in retrospect that it really could have been Chevrolet's intention to replace the beautiful 1963 style Corvette body after only four years of production, but it is certain that the model we now call the 1968 was intended to have been introduced as the 1967. As it turned out, more development work was required on the replacement Corvette, which took its styling cues from the Mako Shark II of 1965, so the new one-piece front bumpered car was delayed until 1968.

How could this Sting Ray model run for only four years when the Corvette has managed more than 40 years on just three chassis and four bodies? The 1953-62 design was modified every two or three years, but maintained its essential wraparound windshield character and dimensions for 10 years. The 1968-82 managed to last 15 years, again with updates every two or three years, but with major components such as doors, flip-up headlights and windshield remaining virtually unchanged. Now the 1984 shape car looks set to run for at least 13 years, and has received fewer styling updates than any other phase in the Corvette's history.

The fabulously desirable 1967 L89 coupe (above), photographed by Jerry Heasley, had aluminum cylinder heads and only 16 were made. A 1967 big-block roadster (facing page) with cast aluminum bolt-on wheels: here at last was an optional wheel that was lighter than the stock steel wheel, due to the loss of the adapter and spinner. Revised five-slot front fender vents were a new feature for '67. Beneath the hood of this 427/400 (right) lurk the famous Tri-power triple two-barrel Holleys under the air cleaner – this car is air conditioned too.

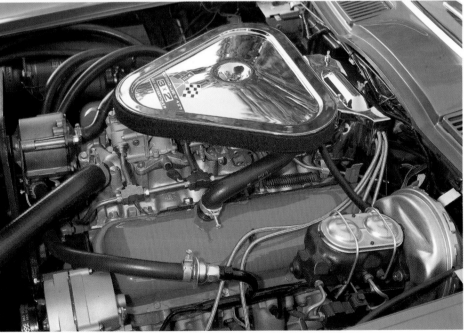

All '67 big-block cars had contrasting color panels on the hood. The color was determined by the choice of interior and exterior finish, and often differed from the interior color. The hood also gained this aggressive fake intake on its bulge.

In the 1950s Corvette production never exceeded 10,000 units annually, and the model was a sleek and unique design that could survive the 10-year production period without the expense of major change. The 1968-82 saw sales peak in 1979 at over 50,000 cars and there was clearly a reluctance to change a successful formula. Recently, the staggering cost of developing new cars and perfecting them to the standards of quality, fit and finish demanded today has meant that all models must have a much longer life.

Detroit was an incredibly exciting place for a car enthusiast to be in the early 1960s. GM had built its magnificent Technical Center at Warren, Michigan, in 1955. Designed by the architect Eero Saarinen, its superb facilities and university campus atmosphere attracted the very best designers and engineers. Within 10 years, GM Styling Staff, under the skilled inspiration of the great Bill Mitchell since 1958, were designing some of the world's most beautiful cars, shifting the epicentre of great car design from Italy to North America.

Throughout this period, each model from each of the five GM divisions was revised annually, with the biggest sellers, the full-size sedans, receiving all-new sheet metal each year. Unfortunately, the demand for annual change in a competitive environment often resulted in lovely designs being ruined for change's sake – just look at what they did to the Buick Riviera and Oldsmobile Toronado in 1968. Against this background, running a Corvette body for only four years is therefore not so surprising.

The mid-period Corvette design was eventually produced for five years. The all-new body that had been designed to fit the 1966 chassis had hit aerodynamic and other problems, so its introduction was postponed by a year, to 1968. The styling staff were therefore presented with the opportunity to do a final refinement on Larry Shinoda's beautiful design for 1967. The result of their work was one of the high points of Corvette production, a car that is today valued as highly as the '63 split-window coupe or the '65 fuel injection.

The body was cleaned up by the removal of the crossed flags from the fenders and the use of new fender louvers with five angled slots behind the front wheels. The small-block hood lost its emblem, so that at last this was a completely clear panel. When fitted with the Mark IV engine, the hood was a new, aggressive design with a fake intake at the front of a bulge that extended back over the cowl area.

When this hood was supplied for the 550bhp plus L88 engine, it was converted to a 'cold air' version at the St Louis assembly plant by cutting two slots at the back to draw high pressure air from the base of the windshield, while a plenum chamber was bonded to the underside to fit snugly over the 850cfm 4150 Holley, sealing to an air cleaner base plate. On lifting this hood, the air cleaner element remained in place inside the plenum. This was the first use by Chevrolet of a ducted remote cold air supply to obtain 'free' horsepower for a carburetor car, by using denser outside air to improve combustion

A 1967 convertible with hard-top on test with *Road & Track* magazine. All '67s have a back-up light above the license plate, and four red tail lights.

within the engine. Previous fuel-injected cars, and all Corvettes since 1973, have used this system in one form or another.

The 1967 big-block hood could not be ordered for the small-block car but was a popular after-market addition for owners of 327s at the time, so modern restorers of these cars have then had to find original plain hoods to replace them and make their cars correct. In Noland Adam's essential *Complete Corvette Restoration & Technical Guide*, published in 1987, it was revealed that the factory fitted big-block hoods to small-block cars for between three and five days at the end of March 1967 because a screwdriver, normally used for releasing the cured 327 hoods, was dropped into the mold, damaging it when it was closed. Once stocks of these 327 hoods were exhausted, the big-block version had to be used until the mold was repaired and supplies of the small-block hoods could be resumed.

On all but the earliest 1967 big-blocks, the hood sported a pair of 427 numerals while the bulge and the spear were painted in a contrasting color, which was determined by the body color and trim combination. For instance, a white car with a red interior would have red hood stripe, while a black car with a saddle interior would have a white hood stripe.

At the back of the car the gas filler door was now body-colored with a metal crossed-flag emblem, replacing the black-painted, metal-framed, clear molded plastic item that had been changed in each of the four

preceding years. Once again there were four active tail lamps, because the back-up lamps which had been located in the inboard rear lamp positions migrated to a new unit above the license plate. Below the doors, the rocker panel covers were new with a blacked-out lower half, while the door step trims were also revised.

Five-slot ventilated steel Rally wheels with a 6in rim replaced the 5½in disc wheels and full covers of previous years. With their small plain center cap and broad outer stainless steel trim ring, these were the start of a 16-year Corvette tradition in standard wheels. The optional aluminum wheel was redesigned as a direct bolt-on, dispensing with the knock-off adapter and saving 8lb of unsprung weight per wheel. New federal regulations for 1967 prohibited projecting trim so the spinners on both the base and optional wheels had to go.

Brakes were also revised for 1967. The parking brake lever, previously next to the steering column, was relocated in the classic sports car position between the seats, although the feeble miniature drums and shoes still precluded European-style handbrake turns. The front and rear brake calipers and pistons were also modified. Each piston originally had a hard plastic insulator secured with a cross-headed screw. In service, particularly in northern areas where the roads were salted in winter, aluminum oxides built up behind the insulator and spalled it off, or the screw rusted through and released the insulator. The 1965-66 pistons were also fitted into guides cast and machined in the back of each caliper chamber. Both of

71

Engine contrasts. The awesome L89 427/435bhp (left), which had aluminum cylinder heads to give a significant weight saving. A more humble 1967 327/300bhp (below) with air conditioning and power brakes.

these features were now deemed unnecessary, so each piston bore directly onto the back of the pad. When remanufacturing the earlier calipers with stainless inserts, the suppliers invariably modify the calipers and use the second design pistons unless requested to do otherwise. The master cylinder was now dual on both power and non-power systems, and included a balance valve and safety warning switch.

Apart from broader-headed control knobs and the loss of the passenger grab handle, the instruments and console were carried over from the previous year. The doors carried neat blue and silver reflective stickers proclaiming 'GM Mark of Excellence'. An interesting new option was the U15 speed-warning speedometer. A sign of the times

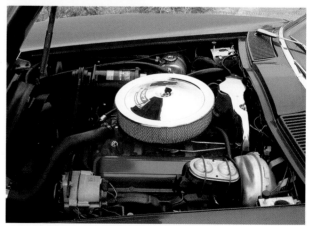

Interior of a 1967 air conditioned roadster (above), showing new position between the seats for the parking brake lever. Removal of hood and side emblems, less aggressive fender vents and simple wheel covers made the '67 a particularly beautiful car (right). This one-owner big-block L71 427/435bhp roadster in Lynndale Blue (below right) lives in England – at last Corvettes are widely appreciated in Europe.

in an increasingly speed-regulated world, where Corvettes were always the focus of the enforcers' attention, this device used a second pointer in the manner of an alarm clock which was set by a knob to buzz when the set speed was exceeded. Discontinued after only three years, the same result can be achieved today in silence with a cruise control.

Under the hood the steering column now incorporated a collapsible section to reduce the risk of injury to the driver in a frontal accident. While the 300bhp small-block remained the base – and most popular – engine choice, options moved further towards the big-block with a choice of no fewer than five 427s against the one L79 350bhp optional small-block.

The 1967 L88, the most powerful motor of them all. With output of around 560bhp, this was intended for racing only. No radiator shroud was fitted, nor a radio – note also the lack of ignition shielding and plug wires with no braid. The air cleaner was built into the cold air hood.

The most popular of the 427s was the 390bhp L36, which breathed through a single Holley with a compression ratio of 10.25:1. Next up was the L68, which used three Holley two-barrels on the same motor to give an extra 10bhp with the same compression ratio. Officially, the most powerful engine was the 435bhp L71, which used the same 'Tri-power' Holley but on an 11.0:1 compression and four-bolt main bearing capped block. To save some weight, this same L71 motor could be supplied with aluminum instead of cast iron cylinder heads and was designated the L89. Not only did they improve the handling and acceleration, but the aluminum heads reduced pre-ignition and improved cooling due to their better conductivity, and could always be repaired no matter how badly damaged.

If there is one Corvette motor that has passed into legend, and is known about by enthusiasts who have no other interest in the cars, it must be the L88. Only 20 were sold in 1967 and only 216 in total by the time production finished in 1969. Officially rated at just 430bhp, the true output was around 560bhp at 6400rpm running on 103 octane gasoline. Although it was among the most powerful engines ever offered in a production car, the '430bhp' rating was stated to discourage the kind of buyers who checked every option box on the order form to ensure that their car was fully loaded. It may even have been intended to fool senior management, who were always aware that the horsepower race could

potentially backfire in litigation and negative publicity, and who had already tried to limit the big-block motor to under 400cu in.

The power output was achieved by a 12.5:1 compression ratio using domed pistons and the L71 aluminum heads, a radical high-lift camshaft with 136 degrees of overlap, and a single Holley 850cfm carburetor on top of an alloy intake manifold with an opened-up plenum. At the bottom end a forged crank, cross-drilled to improve lubrication, was restrained by four-bolt main bearing caps. To make sure that only serious racers ordered the L88, it came with a compulsory list of options: heavy-duty J56 metallic brakes, M22 'rock-crusher' four-speed manual transmission and stiff F41 suspension. Power windows, radio and heater were not available, the last because C48 heater delete was part of the L88 package.

To save weight, and to ensure that the car was not used on the street, the radiator shroud was omitted. Combined with ignition timing set at 12 degrees BTDC, and idle set at 900rpm as specified, this car could never be used in traffic. There was no positive crankcase ventilation system, for a road draft tube was instead hooked dramatically onto the top of the left-hand valve cover. Behind the gear shift was a sticker with a strict message: 'Warning: vehicle must operate on a fuel having a minimum of 103 research octane…or engine damage may result'.

LIVING ON

One of the most appealing aspects of Corvette ownership is the longevity and continuity of the marque. Corvettes have been built continuously for more than half the time that cars have been mass-produced, and are still made in the same two-seater only format as they were at the beginning. Incredibly, this has been achieved with only three chassis during a period of more than 40 years.

If you have a Corvette, any Corvette, you can join a Corvette club or go to a Corvette rally and be proud of your car, because there has never been a dud Corvette. You can have a '65 to restore, drive and show at weekends, and a cheap '85 as an economical, everlasting and convenient weekday commuter and shopper. You could even fit the cylinder heads off a '55 straight onto the '65 or the '85, start up and drive away. Tell that to a Porsche owner! The '63 uses the same A-arms, ball joints, track rod ends, steering box, idler arm, rear trailing arms, rear wheel spindles and more as the '82, which is a full 20 years younger.

There are also his 'n' hers combinations of the same year which are both characterful but completely different. Try a Silver Pearl '67 Coupe 327/300 with powerglide and air against a '67 Convertible 427/435 with M22 four-speed and side-mount exhaust. Maybe you would like a split-window '63 and love to drive 1000 miles a weekend to watch Corvettes race in the vintage series, but cannot live with the two-speed powerglide or a carburetor? Easy, the TH 700 R4 four-speed automatic and tuned port injection will fit right in, you store the 'box and carb somewhere safe, and the car remains 100 per cent Corvette.

As a Corvette specialist who deals with both parts and car sales, I love the constant stimulus and interest bestowed on our hobby by the continued production of new and better models. The '63-67 is a better car simply because we know that there will be another new model next year. The XKE and Austin-Healey annually recede further into their glorious past, but Corvette people can look into the future as well.

It is incredibly easy to buy parts for the Corvette, and GM still carries an amazing range for the Sting Ray. Here again the continuity helps: if Chevrolet had given up the 'Vette in 1973 when crash bumpers and emissions looked set to kill it off, the catalog would now be almost empty. As it is, the Corporation loves its Corvette fans. No other American car has ever commanded such loyalty, and this feel-good factor helps to sell all other Chevrolets as well.

The after-market in restoration parts is vast too. With no limit to the lengths to which restorers will go to

The author drag racing his 1966 L79 327/350bhp in England in 1971. Used daily and driven to the track, it regularly saw off all local opposition.

Trevor Rogers' 1965 Corvette frame after restoration. Even the factory chalk stripes to indicate body shimming have been reproduced. The rear spinner and adapter have since been correctly fitted.

A '67 coupe entering the Corvette Corral at the annual 'Corvettes at Carlisle' meet in Pennsylvania. To buy cars, parts or just look, this is the place to go on the East Coast. The Corvette hobby is now a major industry.

obtain the tiniest part, many start manufacturing for themselves first part-time, and then full-time. NOS (New Old Stock) parts become rarer as they are used up in restorations. When news gets out that GM is about to delete a part, warehouse shelves nationwide are cleared as dealers and restorers stockpile for the future.

Some parts are reproduced so well that they become 'must-have' items for cars that never had them. Knock-off aluminum wheels were never fitted to more than five per cent of '63-66 cars and bolt-on aluminums to barely three per cent of '67s, and yet at any Corvette show probably more than half the mid-year cars will have these wheels. The reason, of course, is that so many Corvettes had custom wheels fitted during the 1960s and '70s. When the time came to return the car to original, the

Remarkable studio view of Sting Ray rolling chassis. The L76 327/365bhp motor is one of the liveliest of the small-blocks. The fan on this car has subsequently been painted the correct black. Radial tires reflect the owner's intention to drive hard upon the car's completion.

optional wheels were the obvious choice. Even these wheels have been subject to evolutionary development. As originally supplied, the GM knock-off wheels had to be hit with a lead hammer to a torque of 450lb ft to be safely tight, and I used to check mine weekly. The spinners soon showed signs of this beating so roll pins were introduced to lock them in place, making these wheels much safer but defeating the original quick-change purpose. Now the suppliers have gone one stage

With rear drive, locking diff and narrow tires, the Corvette is a great car for fun in the snow (above left). Lines of '63-67s at Bloomington, Indiana, for the biggest Mid-West **show (above) that is also the home of the Bloomington Gold judging system, the ultimate test of perfect, factory-correct restoration.**

further and re-designed the wheels so that they can be bolted in place without touching the spinner at all!

The 1963-67 Corvette has survived the intervening years well, but like all classic cars it went through a period of comparative neglect. In the late 1960s and '70s the drum-braked '63-64 cars were spurned by enthusiasts as road cars, because newer Corvettes and most other performance cars by this time had discs. Those who drove '65-67s suffered endless brake problems, or enormous expense, until the invention of the stainless steel sleeved caliper in 1976.

Eight-track and then cassette tape players complete with dual-cone speakers had to be built into any car in the music-mad 1970s, and most were fitted by owners who were enthusiastic with the hacksaw and drill, and eager to twist bare wires into the harness. When these wires chafed and grounded, they cooked wires and insulation in the loom, which would then fail or give intermittent trouble for years. The custom wheel craze saw the fenders of thousands of Sting Rays cut away and then weighed down with filler to make the essential flares. Outer rear wheel bearings and rear spindles then broke up under the strain of the excess offset. A whole generation of drivers grew up thinking that Corvettes were evil handling because all the cars they tried had wacky 50 profile bias-belt tires that made a nonsense of the sophisticated suspension.

The 1963-67 Sting Ray does not have the highest ultimate cornering power (that crown presently rests with the 1984 and newer models), but the 1963-67 is the best handling Corvette of them all when fitted with modern 70 or 75 profile radial tires in equivalent sizes to the originals. A comparison with the '68 and later models is interesting here, particularly because both cars have the

same chassis. The wider wheels and tires of the later cars certainly give more grip, but they lose out in steering feel and feedback. The narrower tires of the early cars break away sooner and control is also easier because of the more upright driving position.

The narrow tires also make the Sting Ray an outstanding snow car. With a non-rusting body, quick throttle response and power to pull low revs in the upper gears, this is a car to drive on the back roads or the empty mall parking lot when the snow is freshly fallen. Keep the top down: the heater is so powerful that you will stay warm. A set of M&S (Mud & Snow) radials will send rooster tails of the cold white powder out behind you, and simultaneously improve your driving skill. In summer, on the other hand, this is the car in which to live those dreams of freedom, keep off the freeway and navigate by the sun.

What really makes the Sting Ray Corvette the great car it is today is hard to sum up, but it has a lot to do with strength and durability combined with an excess of horsepower. The immense and removable chassis, the indestructible and beautiful body, the motor that's still the best after 40 years – all of these combine to make a unique package. But also the Corvette is a testimonial to two maverick car nuts, Zora Arkus-Duntov and Bill Mitchell, who manipulated the biggest Corporation of them all to give us the best sports car of them all.

APPENDIX

As explained in the text, there were a variety of optional engines available for each year. These are summarised below with their RPO (Regular Production Option) numbers. The 1963-65 base motor had no RPO number since it was not an option.

Optional engines

RPO	Size	Bore × stroke	CR	Max bhp at rpm	Carbs	Years
Small-blocks						
L75	327	$4 \times 3\frac{1}{4}$	10.5	300 at 5000	Carter 1×4	63-65
L76	327	$4 \times 3\frac{1}{4}$	11.25	340 at 6000	Carter 1×4	63
L84	327	$4 \times 3\frac{1}{4}$	11.25	360 at 6000	Fuel injection	63
L76	327	$4 \times 3\frac{1}{4}$	11.25	365 at 6200	Holley 1×4	64-65
L84	327	$4 \times 3\frac{1}{4}$	11.25	375 at 6200	Fuel injection	64-65
L79	327	$4 \times 3\frac{1}{4}$	11.0	350 at 5800	Holley 1×4	65-67
L79	327	$4 \times 3\frac{1}{4}$	10.5	300 at 5000	Holley 1×4	66-67
Big-blocks						
L78	396	$4\frac{3}{32} \times 3\frac{49}{64}$	11.0	425 at 6400	Holley 1×4	65
L36	427	$4\frac{1}{4} \times 3\frac{49}{64}$	10.25	390 at 5400	Holley 1×4	66-67
L72	427	$4\frac{1}{4} \times 3\frac{49}{64}$	11.00	425 at 6400	Holley 1×4	66
L68	427	$4\frac{1}{4} \times 3\frac{49}{64}$	10.25	400 at 5400	Holley 3×2	67
L71	427	$4\frac{1}{4} \times 3\frac{49}{64}$	11.00	435 at 5800	Holley 3×2	67
L88	427	$4\frac{1}{4} \times 3\frac{49}{64}$	12.5	430★	Holley 1×4	67

★Official figure, but the true output is believed to be around 560bhp (see page 74).

Production by model year

Year	Coupe	Convertible	Total
1963	10594	10919	21513
1964	8304	13925	22229
1965	8186	15376	23562
1966	9958	17762	27720
1967	8504	14436	22940

Vehicle Identification Numbers

Model year	First	Last
9/62 - 8/63	30837S100001	30837S121513
9/63 - 7/64	40837S100001	40837S122229
8/64 - 8/65	194375S100001	194375S123562
9/65 - 8/66	194376S100001	194376S127720
9/66 - 8/67	194377S100001	194377S122940

The sequential Vehicle Identification Number is found on the reinforcement bar under the passenger's front glovebox. The numbers shown are for coupes – for all convertibles the fourth digit is a 6 instead of a 3.

Technical specifications

1963 Small-block 250bhp
Engine V8 **Construction** Cast iron block and heads **Crankshaft** Five-bearing **Bore and stroke** 4.00in × 3.25in (102.0mm × 82.6mm) **Capacity** 327cu in (5356cc) **Valves** Pushrod ohv **Compression ratio** 10.5:1 **Fuel system** Mechanical fuel pump, one four-barrel Carter carburetor **Maximum power** 250bhp at 4400rpm **Maximum torque** 350lb ft at 2800rpm **Transmission** Three- or four-speed manual, or two-speed automatic **Final drive ratio** 3.36:1 standard, 3.08:1 optional **Top gear per 1000rpm** 23.1mph **Brakes** 11.0in drums front and rear, servo optional **Front suspension** Independent with wishbones, coil springs, telescopic dampers and anti-sway bar **Rear suspension** Independent by trailing arms and lower transverse rods, U-jointed half shafts acting as upper locating links, transverse leaf spring, telescopic dampers **Steering** Recirculating ball, 17.6:1 ratio, power assistance optional **Wheels & tires** 5.5 × 15 steel with 6.70 × 15 tires **Wheelbase** 98.0in (2489mm) **Length** 175.3in (4453mm) **Width** 69.6in (1768mm) **Curb weight** 3160lb (1433kg) **Maximum speed** 130mph **Maximum speed in gears** First, 65mph; second, 88mph; third, 110mph; fourth, 130mph **Typical fuel consumption** 18mpg (US)

1967 Big-block 435bhp
As above except as follows: **Bore and stroke** 4.25in × 3.76in (108.0mm × 95.5mm) **Capacity** 427cu in (7000cc) **Compression ratio** 11.0:1 **Fuel system** Mechanical fuel pump, three two-barrel Holley carburetors **Maximum power** 435bhp at 5800rpm **Maximum torque** 460lb ft at 4000rpm **Transmission** Four-speed manual **Final drive ratio** 3.55:1, Positraction standard **Top gear per 1000rpm** 22.2mph **Brakes** 11.75in ventilated discs with four-piston calipers, servo optional **Rear suspension** Anti-sway bar added **Wheels & tires** 6 × 15 with 7.75 × 15 tires **Curb weight** 3400lb (1542kg) **Maximum speed** 145mph **Typical fuel consumption** 15mpg (US)

ACKNOWLEDGEMENTS

Grateful thanks are due to the owners in the USA who allowed their cars to be photographed by Berle Cherney specially for this book: they are Ron Goralski (1963 and 1964 coupes) and Mike McCagh (1965 coupe and big-block convertible). Fred Mullauer, ace Corvette restorer, kindly provided guidance for this photographic work. Further special color photography in the USA came from Jerry Heasley and David Fetherston. Our principal source of archive photographs was Ludvigsen Associates (thanks to distinguished Corvette author Karl Ludvigsen and Christine Lalla) of London. Author Tom Falconer and his UK-based company, Claremont Corvette, provided valuable historic photographs in color and black and white. In addition other photographs were provided by General Motors, *Road & Track* magazine (thanks to Otis Meyer), Bob Tronolone (Sting Ray racer shots from Riverside), *Classic and Sportscar* magazine (thanks to Charlie Pierce, Mick Walsh and Carol Page), Trevor Rogers (body-off studio shots), *Vette Vues* magazine, Nick Baldwin, David Hodges and Terry Simms.